D0459250

YEARBOOK
2002

THE YEAR IN
REVIEW 2001

People weekly

contents

yearbook staff

editor: Elizabeth Sporkin

senior editor: Richard Burgheim

art director: Joseph Cavalieri

associate editor: Allison Adato

chief of reporters: Randy Vest

picture editor: Brian Belovitch

researchers: P.J. Murray, David Lewis

copy editor: Tommy Dunne

operations: Helen Russell

© copyright 2001 Time Inc. Home Entertainment
published by

People Books®

a division of Time Inc., 1271 Avenue of the Americas
New York, New York 10020

president: Rob Gursha
vice president, branded businesses: David Arfine
executive director, marketing services: Carol Pittard
director, retail & special sales: Tom Mifsud
director, finance: Tricia Griffin
marketing director: Kenneth Maehlum
product manager: Dennis Sheehan
editorial operations manager: John Calvano
associate product manager: Sara Stumpf
assistant product manager: Linda Frisbie

ISSN: 1522-5895
ISBN: 1-929049-63-3

People Books is a trademark of Time Inc.

All rights reserved. No part of this book may be reproduced in any form or by any electronic or mechanical means, including information storage and retrieval systems, without permission in writing from the publisher, except by a reviewer, who may quote brief passages in a review.

We welcome your comments and suggestions about People Books. Please write to us at: People Books, Attention: Book Editors, PO Box 11016, Des Moines, IA 50336-1016

If you would like to order any of our hardcover Collector's Edition books, please call us at 1-800-327-6388 (Monday through Friday, 7:00 a.m.- 8:00 p.m. or Saturday, 7:00 a.m.-6:00 p.m. Central Time). Please visit our Web site at www.TimeBookstore.com.

special thanks to: Jane Bealer, Robert Britton, Lisa Burnett, Sal Covarrubias, Suzanne DeBenedetto, Urbano DelValle, Robert Dente, Gina Di Meglio, Tom Fitzgibbon, Sally Foster, Margery Frohlinger, Peter Harper, George Hill, Patricia Hustoo, Lance Kaplan, Salvador Lopez, Natalie McCrea, Jessica McGrath, Dot McMahon, Maddy Miller, Eric Mischel, Gregory Monfries, Charles Nelson, Jonathan Polsky, Emily Rabin, Susan Radlauer, Mikema Reape, Mary Jane Rigoroso, Annette Rusin, Steven Sandonato, Barbara Scott, Meredith Shelley, John A. Silva, Bozena Szwagulinski, Ann Tortorelli, Janell Umemoto, Marina Weinstein, Niki Whelan, Céline Wojtala, Patrick Yang, Peter Zambouros

PRINTED IN THE UNITED STATES OF AMERICA

6

After the World Trade Center attacks, President Bush showed his support at Ground Zero.

140

Paul McCartney and Ringo Starr mourned a "baby brother" and "best friend."

86

The Academy honored Benicio Del Toro and Marcia Gay Harden.

STORIES
OF THE YEAR

Cover

HEARTS WIDE SHUT

Cover

With family, a multimillion-dollar fortune and pride on the line, Tom Cruise's blunt divorce petition suggests he'll be playing the tough guy

CRUISING FOR CONTROL

Part P.T. Barnum, part doting mom, Madonna—with nannies, tots, a spouse, 265 costumes and a mechanical bull in tow—barnstorms America. Yee-haa, indeed

Balancing Act

Diva in Distress

Beset by work pressures and romantic troubles, Mariah Carey breaks down

Cover

The First Lady Next Door

A small-town girl with no consuming passion for politics, Laura Bush brings to the White House unaffected charm, quiet humor and a confident personal style

Cover

Dismayed with the drinking life, Ben Affleck enters rehab to get back on track

Reality Check

HELL ON EARTH

In New York City, those who escaped the carnage ran a horrifying gauntlet

Cover

Breaking the Silence

At long last, Congressman Gary Condit goes public. But he leaves as many mysteries as he solves

Bitter February brought a **very public split** to a much watched celeb marriage. In spring we cheered Julia's big night. And Madonna lit up our summer on the road with her brood. But as the fall chill approached, a **horrific tragedy** unfolded, making us long for a time when a divorce, an Oscar or a rock tour could be the biggest headline of the day

SEPTEMBER

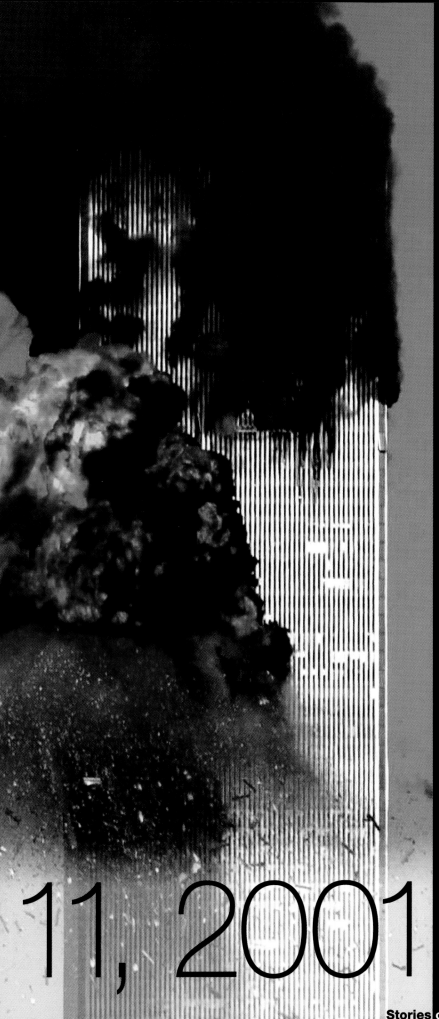

A single day shattered the sense of security America had taken for granted.

Now we were a nation at war against terrorism

Within 54 minutes, terrorists had hit the Twin Towers of New York City's World Trade Center and the Pentagon (above) in the capital, leaving images that would forever sear the American psyche.

11, 2001

America Rallies

The 2,400° heat melted the buildings' steel infrastructure. It was, said a witness, "the most nightmarish thing you ever saw."

Some who escaped the falling towers were injured in the stampede away from the volcanic dust storm that followed.

Defense Secretary Donald Rumsfeld refused to leave the Pentagon, even after 125 were killed in the southwest wing.

"It was snowing debris," said a Wall Street worker. "A cloud of ash overcame us. It was pitch-black. You could not see your hands."

Just a few blocks from the Trade Center, Stuyvesant High School students were among the youngest evacuees.

FOUR HIJACKINGS BRING SHOCK AND UNBEARABLE GRIEF

For many New Yorkers the day began with a consummate, if mundane, expression of their rights as citizens in a free society: They voted. Polls opened at 6 a.m. so that people could pick a mayoral candidate between kissing their kids goodbye at school and heading to work. They might be excused for dawdling, as the city was enjoying a gorgeous late summer day. It was sunny, in fact, over much of the East Coast. A perfect day for flying.

At 8:00 a.m., American Airlines Flight 11 left Boston's Logan Airport for Los Angeles. Fourteen minutes later, United Flight 175, also bound for L.A., departed Logan. At 8:21, American 77 took off for L.A. from Washington Dulles Airport. And at 8:42, United 93 left Newark for San Francisco. As the world shortly learned, none of those planes, nor the 265 passengers and crew, would reach their intended destinations. At 8:47, American 11 slammed into the north tower of New York's World Trade Center. Anyone who believed the crash a horrific accident knew differently when, at 9:02, United 175 quite deliberately pierced the second tower. On board, hijackers armed with knives and box cutters had taken over the aircraft and turned them into manned missiles. Both towers stood burning, as thousands of occupants scrambled in chaos to escape while several battalions of firefighters rushed in. At 9:41, when American 77 nose-dived into the Pentagon, these events seemed nothing less than a declaration of war. Meanwhile, on United 93, passengers were waging their own battle against the hijackers. One phoned out to say, "I know we're going to die. Some of us are going to do something about it." They did lose their lives in a Pennsylvania field but saved many more by preventing the plane from hitting a populated target, possibly the White House.

George W. Bush was at a Florida grade school that morning when Chief of Staff Andrew Card whispered in his ear. Upon hearing of the second crash, the President blanched, then composed himself and told the kids they were "really good readers." Shortly thereafter Bush declared, "This is a difficult time for America," and launched a mission to "hunt down the folks who committed this act."

The first body taken from the site was that of fire department chaplain Mychal Judge, who was killed by debris while performing last rites.

A STAGGERING DEATH TOLL RISES

"It looked like the end of the world," said an office worker in lower Manhattan. At 9:50 the south tower of the World Trade Center began to fall, its girders liquefied by the explosion. At 10:28 the north tower followed, contributing to the deadliest day—some 4,000 presumed killed—on U.S. soil since the Civil War. New York City mayor Rudolph Giuliani, predicting a final toll "more than anyone can bear," sealed off the city. Bridges and tunnels closed. Subways stopped. Schools let out early. In Washington the White House, Capitol and other federal buildings were evacuated. Nationwide, airports closed, and all 30,000 flights were grounded for the first time in history. Disneyland emptied. The baseball season was temporarily put on hold. Only near the disaster sites did activity increase. In New York thousands of emergency workers—firefighters, police, medics—tore toward a scene from which everyone else was fleeing. Feeling helplessly unoccupied, throngs of people turned out at hospitals to donate blood. But as survivors rescued from the World Trade Center wreckage became scarcer, volunteers were sent home and blood banks declared themselves beyond capacity. Numb, many people stayed home watching the ghastly events play out again and again and again on television.

The fire at the World Trade Center—fueled by a sunken heap of carpets, computers, furniture and oil reservoirs—still smoldered more than two months after the attacks. The stench of burning debris wafted over the city, a constant reminder of the tragedy.

America Rallies

A dusting of ash blanketed numerous Battery Park–area apartments. Many were structurally compromised and evacuated.

Like many of his peers, Jerry Reilly of Engine Co. 76 worked despite his grief, after the death of 343 firefighters.

In addition to New York's two tallest buildings, the attacks destroyed or severely damaged numerous other structures.

America Rallies

"Life presents as many opportunities for happiness as it does for tragedy," said Giuliani at the Yankee Stadium service.

New York colleagues offer a final salute to fire chaplain Judge. Firefighters from across the U.S. also came to pay homage.

Posted in hope of finding loved ones, handmade missing flyers soon became haunting tributes to the presumed dead.

New Yorkers brought firehouses flowers, candles and more. "Trays of lasagna, fruit baskets," marveled one fireman. "It's an incredible feeling."

Union Square hosted New York's largest candlelit shrine. After the first rain, snapshots appeared streaked by tears.

SOMBERLY, WE PRAYED AND REMEMBERED

"Maybe this ceremony will give us some closure," said a mourner at a World Trade Center vigil. "But I don't think so. I think this is going to last a long time." Its psychic wounds were still raw, but the nation came together to do what needed to be done. We eulogized the dead, uttered prayers of comfort and began to find a place for the tragedy in our history. On September 14, the President offered condolences at Washington's National Cathedral. His sentiments echoed in services across the country, many of which were interfaith. "We are neighbors, we are family members, we are friends—and we are hurt," said Imam Izak-El Mu'eed Pasha, a Muslim NYPD chaplain. Added Rabbi Joseph Potasnik, a Jewish FDNY chaplain: "We have become the Reunited States of America." Some were at a loss for what to pray for. One woman asked simply that God show a sign of existence.

Oprah Winfrey and James Earl Jones turned Yankee Stadium into a massive house of worship, leading a memorial with performances from Bette Midler and Plácido Domingo. Also on hand was Rudy Giuliani, 57. The mayor seemed to appear at every service in the city that week, in between overseeing relief efforts, calming a jittery populace and talking up the city to the rest of America. His efforts made fans of the prickly mayor's erstwhile enemies, including Hillary Clinton and Governor George Pataki. *The Washington Post* called him "Winston Churchill in a Yankees cap." By the time Queen Elizabeth II knighted Giuliani, he had transcended politics to become a folk hero. Declared the mayor, humbled for the first time in memory: "I am in absolute awe of the incredible strength of the people of this city. I have seen the worst things I've ever seen in my life, and I have seen the best."

After delivering remarks at the National Cathedral, the President received a "well done" pat on the hand from his father.

Homeowners in Kaukauna, Wisconsin, turned their lawn into a Rockwellian display.

Americans flaunted their patriotism from sea to shining sea, including in this park in New York's Greenwich Village.

America Rallies

With so few remains found in the wreckage, mourners received urns filled with soil from New York's Ground Zero.

President Bush used the hard-bitten lingo of movie westerns to describe the hunt for bin Laden. Visual aids soon followed.

An anthrax-tainted letter sent to NBC (top) infected Erin O'Connor, assistant to anchor Tom Brokaw. After a similar envelope arrived in Senator Tom Daschle's office, at least 28 people on Capitol Hill tested positive for exposure to the deadly toxin.

An American special operations soldier patrolled Khwaja Bahuaddin, a Northern Alliance stronghold in Afghanistan.

Tammy Cross of Florida sent fiancé Sergeant Peter Domoracki, an Army reservist, into active duty with a hug.

THE U.S. FIGHTS TERRORISM AND TREPIDATION

All 19 hijackers were dead. But al-Qaeda, the network to which they likely belonged, remained. Once intelligence sources confirmed that Osama bin Laden, 44, masterminded the attacks, President Bush acted on his threat to treat nations harboring terrorists as culpable as the terrorists themselves. On October 7 bombs began to fall on Afghanistan, where bin Laden, a Saudi exile, was based. After the President stated that America was not at war with Afghans—food aid was air-dropped in the countryside—bombs blasted the Taliban rulers. Troops followed to support the rebel Northern Alliance.

The enemy at home was fear. People approached their mailboxes with rubber gloves after anthrax-poisoned letters killed five. Members of the U.S. House evacuated—something that had never occurred in any previous war. Meanwhile, trips were canceled for fear of flying, despite the promise of armed marshals on board. Airlines reinforced cockpit doors and replaced metal knives on meal trays with plastic. Lisa Beamer, widowed when her husband, Todd, was killed on United Flight 93, aided the effort by boarding that same flight one month later, saying, "It's time to start getting on with life."

There was encouragement from dramatic developments in Afghanistan. Six weeks after the first bombs, the capital, Kabul, fell. As the Taliban fled, Afghans threw off the constraints of theocratic tyranny. Men queued at barbershops to shave beards they'd been forced to grow. Tentatively, women removed burqas, turning uncovered faces to the sun for the first time in five years. Radios played, children flew kites—both banned activities under the Taliban. There was progress, but, as Vice President Dick Cheney warned the world, "the struggle can end only with [the terrorists'] complete and permanent destruction."

Bush's September 14 visit to the Trade Center site was met with rousing cheers of "USA, USA" from emergency workers.

Marine corpsmen demonstrated anthrax cleanup techniques at a news conference outside the Capitol.

Back in the spotlight with a new album, Michael Jackson headlined the United We Stand benefit concert at D.C.'s RFK Stadium.

At the L.A. wing of the three-city Heroes telethon, Goldie Hawn took pledges on her phone—and on Kurt Russell's.

SOME FAMOUS FACES JOIN COUNTLESS VOLUNTEERS

If anything positive came of the events on September 11, it was the groundswell of altruism. Haute New York eateries fed rescue workers. Massage therapists gave free rubdowns to cleanup crews. Many celebs did their bit. Kathleen Turner aided dispatchers at New York's St. Vincent's hospital. Steve Buscemi rejoined the Manhattan fire company to which he once belonged and pulled victims from the debris.

Most stars did what they do best in a crisis: brought donors to their TV sets and to the phones. A September 21 telethon—in which callers might have reached Jack Nicholson or Meg Ryan taking pledges—raised more than $250 million for the United Way. Money flowed also at benefits held in New York City and Washington, D.C. At the former, crowds cheered a reunion of The Who but booed Richard Gere's suggestion that America practice compassion rather than revenge against our attackers.

With the rest of us, entertainers felt their way through unfamiliar territory. While films with terrorist themes, including Arnold Schwarzenegger's *Collateral Damage,* were postponed, Defense Department staffers met with screenwriters to conjure possible future attack scenarios. Instructed to go back to work by President Bush and Mayor Giuliani, David Letterman led the pack in New York. Baseball resumed, culminating in an emotional World Series. Bill Maher was lambasted for wondering if suicide bombers were braver than pilots lobbing missiles from afar. But Ellen DeGeneres got an approving laugh at the Emmys, asking, "What would bug the Taliban more than seeing a gay woman in a suit surrounded by Jews?" One answer: Seeing Americans resolve to live as they had on September 10.

Paul McCartney wrote a song, "Freedom," after the terror attacks and sang it at the New York benefit.

Leonardo DiCaprio and Robert De Niro helped raise $30 million for the Robin Hood fund to aid N.Y.C. victims' families.

Shedding his steely facade, newsman Dan Rather broke down in tears during a conversation with David Letterman, the first late-night talk host on the air after September 11.

Nathan Lane took to the streets to proclaim his love of New York and to revive Broadway theater attendance.

At Ground Zero, Robin Williams chatted with recovery workers and, at their request, placed cell phone calls to their wives.

Mick Jagger and Keith Richards rocked for heroes, widows and donors at the Madison Square Garden event.

Parking his cowboy boots at the White House, George W. Bush bids happy trails to the Clinton era

Early into his presidency, George W. Bush faced a challenge when his twin daughters Jenna and Barbara, 20, were cited for underage drinking at a restaurant in Austin near the University of Texas, where Jenna is a sophomore. (Barbara attends Yale.) A reformed drinker himself, Bush, 55, had reluctantly disclosed during the campaign that years ago he was slapped with a DUI. And this was a candidate who repeatedly reminded voters that he would "restore dignity to the White House." So the day he and his wife, Laura, disciplined the girls "was not," said a staffer, "a Kodak moment."

Rebuilding prestige was a work in progress. Bush strove to establish a more disciplined operational style than that of his predecessor. In the early months, before the terrorist attacks, it was a 9-to-5 presidency. Unlike Clinton and his young wonks, who argued policy into the wee hours, Bush implemented M.B.A. efficiency, knocked off early to catch a ball game on TV and hit the sack by 10 p.m. He resurrected trusted advisers from the Reagan and first Bush administrations and never offered up his wife as an unofficial cabinet member. Though Laura, 55, a teacher and librarian, had helped pass an education bill in Austin, she planned to be a more traditional First Lady. "I have the best wife for the line of work I'm in," said Bush. "She doesn't try to steal the limelight."

The crucible of unanticipated horror transformed a President who in previous years had mistaken the Taliban for a band and couldn't name the president of Pakistan. Now, long days were required in the Oval Office, and weekend trips to the ranch were out. Laura Bush took over the President's weekly radio address one Saturday to speak out on the plight of Afghan women. And the former governor and baseball executive proved himself increasingly adept at international summitry, building a crucial rapport with Russian president Putin as well as with Pervez Musharraf, Pakistan's president. While some cringed at his folksy talk of "smoking out" the al-Qaeda as if they were rabbits in the Texas brush, the vast majority came to admire how he rallied the nation. Within two weeks his approval rating soared to 90 percent—the highest ever. Sometime in the twilight of September 11, George W. Bush emerged as our President.

Familiar faces in the Bush II war room include Secretary of State Colin Powell, V.P. Dick Cheney and Joint Chiefs chairman Gen. Henry Shelton.

Jenna and Barbara craved privacy.

Laura says she's only "interested in politics because my husband is."

HERE COME

A President who lost the popular tally came a long way in a year. As Mayor Giuliani declared in New York, "This city—it didn't vote for you—is in love with you."

S THE SON

BEHIND THE
SMILE

After she finally nabbed the little gold guy,
Julia Roberts lost the real man in her life

Comedian Steven Wright once joked, "You can't have everything—where would you put it?" America's $20 million actress tested the theory in 2001, when, for a gold-plated moment, she seemed to have it all. She picked up eight statuettes for her work in *Erin Brockovich,* including the biggie that had twice eluded her: Oscar. But as Roberts, 34, reminded us each time she took the podium, all the success in the world means nothing "if there's not somebody there to say, 'Have a good day, honey.' Benjamin Bratt does that for me." If that smile weren't so disarming, even her most loyal fans might recoil from all of Roberts's good fortune. Instead, they have bought up more than $1.5 billion in tickets to her films and gleefully followed the ups and downs of her romantic life.

To Roberts, and the world, Bratt, 38, seemed like a keeper. As she grinned uncontrollably while talking about the former *Law & Order* star, one could only feel happy for a woman who had endured relentless public scrutiny as she skidded from on-set trysts to canceled nuptials to a brief marriage to Lyle Lovett. But somehow the tabloids, the fans and even their friends missed the cues that the almost-four-year Roberts-Bratt union was in trouble. In June, while promoting *America's Sweethearts* (a film about the secret split of a movie-star couple), Roberts hid heartache: She and Bratt had separated a month earlier. Those close to the couple speculated that his traditional ways—he wanted a family and a home base—conflicted with her desire to put off having kids and to move

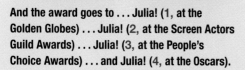

And the award goes to . . . Julia! (1, at the Golden Globes) . . . Julia! (2, at the Screen Actors Guild Awards) . . . Julia! (3, at the People's Choice Awards) . . . and Julia! (4, at the Oscars).

"She went out of her way not to make him feel like Mr. Julia Roberts," said producer friend Howard Rosenman of Bratt. Below: Roberts with his successor, Moder.

At a press do for *America's Sweethearts* (with Catherine Zeta-Jones, John Cusack and Billy Crystal), Roberts defined life as "choices, compromises and sacrifices."

where the work took her. But rumors swirled about her *Ocean's 11* costar George Clooney, who denied any involvement, cracking, "I've been too busy breaking up Tom and Nicole." Roberts took such gossip in stride. "To complain about that," she said, "is to be like the fastest woman runner on the planet and complain about a blister." As for having love in tandem with blinding success? By fall Roberts was giving it another try—with Danny Moder, 32, a cameraman she met while shooting *The Mexican*.

Speculation as to what caused Carey's breakdown ranged from an ended romance with singer Luis Miguel to career sabotage from her ex, Tommy Mottola, to distress that her new album and film were commercial duds. The only public explanation from the singer was "exhaustion."

STARS ON THE BRINK

Addicted or just addled, Mariah Carey and others fight for sobriety and repose

Days before she checked into a hospital after suffering an emotional breakdown, Mariah Carey spoke to the press about her new album and first movie. "The title, *Glitter,*" she explained, "is like, you know, everything looks great from the outside." Yes, we know. Everything did look great for Carey. She had freed herself from a contract with Columbia Records, owned by her ex-husband, Tommy Mottola, and signed a five-year, $117 million deal with Virgin Records. But all was not right. At a July record-store appearance Carey, 32, ranted nonsensically, prompting her publicist to yank the mike out of her hand and instruct cameras to stop rolling. The day of her hospitalization she had a tantrum in a hotel room, breaking pottery and reportedly walking across the broken shards. "I don't know what's going on with my life," she wrote on her fan Web site. "I'm gonna be taking some time off."

She was not alone. Matthew Perry briefly halted production of *Friends* and the film *Servicing Sara* in order to get his Vicodin habit under control. Robert Downey Jr., who in January won a Golden Globe for his work on *Ally McBeal,* was later relieved of his duties there when he violated his 1996 parole with a cocaine bust. *The West Wing* creator Aaron Sorkin also nabbed not only a cabinet full of awards but a drug-possession arrest and a mandatory stint in rehab. Battling problems with alcohol, both Backstreet Boy

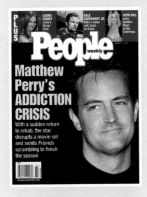

A.J. McLean and Ben Affleck took time to kick the bottle. And Paula Poundstone pleaded no contest to endangering her foster children with a drinking problem, for which she sought help under a court order.

One person who never spun through the revolving door of any rehab unit was Mariah Carey. Shortly after her hospital stay, she gallantly performed at both the Tribute to Heroes telethon and D.C.'s United We Stand benefit. A star since her teens who rarely took a break, Carey got support in and out of the industry. "She's a talented musician and a wonderful girl," said designer Tommy Hilfiger. "For her to be down was so wrong."

▲ "It's like I have a shotgun in my mouth and I've got my finger on the trigger" is how Downey, 36, explained his trouble with drugs to a judge.

▲ "My drinking helped to create a dangerous situation for the children," said Poundstone, 42, who was cleared of lewd-conduct charges.

▲ A 30-day residential drug program, his second go-around, got Perry, 32, out in time for Chandler to marry Monica on the *Friends* finale.

▲ "This has been a public nightmare for me," said Sorkin, 40, of his April possession arrest and use of marijuana and crack cocaine.

▲ When his dependency on alcohol became too much, Affleck, 29, knew who to call: Charlie Sheen, who set him up at a rehab center in Malibu.

▲ After a successful detox, McLean, 23, treated Backstreet Boys shows like AA meetings, announcing how many days' sobriety he had behind him.

MADGE'S

With her family—and nannies—in tow, **Madonna** tours for the first time as a mom

In the song that opened some of the 48 shows of her summer tour, Madonna sang these lines: "I traded fame for love, without a second thought . . . and now I find I've changed my mind." Having enjoyed two decades of monumental fame (not to mention massive fortune), Madonna appeared now to strive for balance. She began 2001 as a newlywed, having married British film director Guy Ritchie (below, *en famille* in New York) the previous December, a day after they christened their 4-month-old son Rocco. As such, her tour—notable for its springboard sets, *Crouching Tiger, Hidden Dragon* flying rigs and a kimono with 52-foot sleeves—was also a family affair. A playroom traveled from venue to venue, a perk for Rocco and Lourdes, Madonna's 5-year-old daughter with ex-boyfriend Carlos Leon, who was often in attendance backstage. Though she kept up with her yoga classes and found time for guitar lessons (she played for the first time onstage), Madonna said in August, "There isn't a second in my day that isn't taken up looking after my family or thinking about my show." When the production, which netted an estimated $50 million in U.S. ticket sales alone, was rumored to be her last, Madonna, 43, denied she was ready to hang up her rhinestone chaps. But a month later, after the September 11 attacks, a source close to the singer said she "can't see herself going back onstage for an international tour again." Taking time off in the fall, she inadvertently landed back in the headlines with the publication of biographer Andrew Morton's book, which probed into the star's liaisons with ex-lovers from Vanilla Ice to Dennis Rodman. It seemed a particularly cynical undertaking, given that Madge, as Ritchie likes to call her and the London press has picked up on, now projects a happy-at-last image of a wife and mother. At the height of her hectic year, pop's Queen Mum declared, "I feel very blessed."

ROAD TRIP

"Next to [her family], I'm probably hoping to find Chandra more than anyone else," said Condit (ducking photographers in July).

KNOW?

A missing intern put the spotlight on **Gary Condit** until a bigger story deflected the glare

A May 1 e-mail to her parents about her plans to attend USC's graduation and pick up her master's degree in person is the last anyone heard from Chandra Levy. Soon after, the 24-year-old Justice Department intern disappeared. After a call from Levy's concerned parents, Robert and Susan, from their Modesto, California, home, D.C. police searched her apartment. They found it in perfect order—packed suitcase, purse and credit cards still there—and no sign of a struggle. In another attempt to locate her daughter, Susan Levy dialed a number that appeared some 20 times on Chandra's phone records. It rang the pager of California congressman Gary Condit.

In the weeks that followed, Condit, 53, a married seven-term Democrat from Modesto, disavowed any knowledge of the circumstances of Levy's disappearance. Yes, he said, he did know her. She was, in his words, a "good friend." That was what he told the police in his first two interviews. But Levy's family suspected more. Her aunt Linda Zamsky recalled Chandra talking about an affair, saying that she believed Condit would leave his wife in order to marry her within five years.

In his third police interview, Condit came forth with an admission: He and Chandra had been lovers, a fact he hoped to conceal from his wife of 34 years, Carolyn, 53, and their children Chad, 34, and Cadee, 26. "I love [Carolyn] very much," said Condit. "I'll stay with her as long as she'll have me."

Carolyn Condit did not appear ready to leave her husband, even as another woman, flight attendant Anne Marie Smith, claimed to have had a 10-month affair with Condit, which he allegedly asked her to lie about.

His stalling and evasiveness, which was by then seen as hindering the hunt for Levy, also fueled a media obsession. Reluctantly Condit cooperated with police, giving a DNA sample and opening his D.C. home to be searched. But asked to take a polygraph, he arranged a private lie-detector test instead. More damaging was his refusal to apologize for his earlier opaqueness. His limited answers to press queries, particularly in a widely seen August interview with ABC's Connie Chung, made Condit look like Lewinsky-era Clinton at his worst: All lawyer-speak, but without the President's lip-biting con-

trition. The Democratic leader in the House, Dick Gephardt, said, "I can't believe he's not taking responsibility."

Then, suddenly, press attention turned from the Condit case to focus on the fall terrorist attacks. By November he appeared ready to announce a run for an eighth term. "We're the underdog in a big way," said son Chad Condit. While some may believe it was purely bad luck that a woman Condit had had an affair with later vanished, others feel his credibility and career ended with the controversy. "A lot of things did change on September 11, for everybody except Gary Condit," noted Democratic consultant Gale Kaufman. "Unfortunately Chandra Levy is still missing."

Did religion split Nicole and Tom? (She was raised Catholic, he's a Scientologist.) Or geography? (She likes Australia, he prefers the U.S.) Kidman reportedly believes Penélope Cruz (above) is the more likely culprit in ending the marriage.

THE $300M BREAKUP

After 10 years, power couple **Tom** and **Nicole** call it quits, as his latest costar becomes his new lady

Like most Tom Cruise vehicles, this one was a blockbuster. In February, Cruise, 39, and wife Nicole Kidman, 34, announced they had separated. Within weeks it came out that he was dating *Vanilla Sky* costar Penélope Cruz, 27. While her husband was the bigger box-office draw, in this drama Kidman had the better lines: "Now I can wear heels," she quipped about life after her three-inches-shorter soon-to-be ex.

Although Cruise stated in his divorce petition that the couple had been married nine years and 11 months, they had, in fact, celebrated their 10th anniversary on Christmas Eve 2000 by renewing their vows before friends in L.A. The discrepancy is likely an attempt to avoid giving half his assets to Kidman, as California law mandates for marriages of a decade or more. Their fortune—including three homes and a private plane once called Sweet Nic, now named Sweet Bella, for their daughter—is estimated at over $300 million.

After the split, their lives became two well-choreographed solos. A planned Fiji vacation was divided: Kidman arrived the first week with kids Isabella, 9, and Connor, 6, while Cruise showed up with Cruz for the second. At the premiere of *The Others,* which Cruise coproduced and Kidman starred in, both took the red carpet, but 20 minutes apart to avoid seeing one another.

Tom, who sought joint custody of his two children, picked up Isabella from ballet class. Steven Spielberg called him a "total dad."

CELL MATE

Biologist James Thomson finds his work thrust under an ethical microscope

Three years ago, the University of Wisconsin's James Thomson, 43, became the first researcher to cultivate human stem cells, primordial cells that can develop into various materials in the body—nerves, blood, brain tissue. More significantly, they hold the potential to treat diseases from Parkinson's to cancer. The extremely shy molecular biologist accepted his field's accolades, then went back to where he was most comfortable: the lab. So it was jolting to suddenly find himself at the center of a national debate. Even as understanding of stem cells' promise spread, so did controversy over their source: They are most often extracted from surplus embryos created for in vitro fertilization. If not implanted to begin a pregnancy, the embryos are discarded. Thomson long ago sorted out his own moral stance. If the cells might be put to scientific use, he concluded, "I could not see that throwing them out was better." The issue was thornier for

President George Bush, who had to decide whether research on stem cells should be federally funded and to weigh the pleas of scientists and patient advocates like Christopher Reeve versus the right-to-life voices including Pope John Paul II. Surprisingly, pro-lifers like Senator Strom Thurmond, differentiating between cells in a petri dish and a fetus in the womb, favored funding the research. And polls showed that 57 percent of abortion opponents supported stem cell research. In August, trying to play political Solomon, Bush ruled that funding would continue for existing stem cell lines, "where the life-and-death decision has already been made," but would not be granted to harvest new lines. Neither side was totally pleased. Researchers worried about access to the limited number of lines (just 72), while funding opponents could hardly be satisfied knowing that experiments would continue on what they believed were lost lives. Thomson, who is married with two children and spends his days in a privately financed lab, reassured allies that "the field will go forward." His own work certainly will. Said colleague Jon Ordorico: "I'm sure Jamie would just like to crawl back into his hole and do science. He wasn't made for this event."

TOO WILD KINGDOM

A spate of **shark** attacks churns up fear in the water

In 2000 there were 79 unprovoked shark attacks worldwide—10 were fatal. By late 2001 there were only 52 and three deaths, but a sudden rash of incidents made it seem as if the finned predators ruled the beaches. In July sharks confronted humans off California, New York, Hawaii and Florida, where Jessie Arbogast, 8, lost an arm to a bull shark. Miraculously, the boy survived blood loss that stopped his heart for 30 minutes; his missing limb was pried from the shark's jaws and re-attached. In September, David Peltier, 10, died from a sandbar shark bite off Virginia Beach. Two days later a shark

This shark, which struck Arbogast (below), was killed by a National Park ranger.

killed a North Carolina man and severely injured his girlfriend. To quell the hysteria, experts published statistics to put the risk into perspective. For instance, a person is more likely to be killed by lightning than by a shark. Even *Jaws* author Peter Benchley spoke out. Despite his dramatization of sharks as hunting humans, he said, "now we know that except in the rarest instances, great white shark attacks are mistakes."

DOMESTIC TRIAL

What made Andrea Yates kill her five children?

Yates (with a sheriff's deputy) pleaded not guilty by reason of insanity. Husband Russell (right) stood by her.

On a June morning Andrea Yates called her NASA engineer husband, Russell, 36, at his Houston office. Her tone made him suspect something was wrong. He asked if anyone was hurt. "Yes," she reportedly replied. "The children. All of them." Before placing that somber call, Yates had drowned the couple's daughter and four sons in a bathtub. Yates, 37, had a history of severe postpartum depression and two suicide attempts. She said she heard voices and believed she was Satan. Her additional, more pedestrian stresses—Yates was homeschooling their five children and caring for her dying father—may have pushed her over the edge. In

jail, Yates was found competent to stand trial for murder after finally receiving the medical attention she needed. "I've never seen her this happy," said her brother Andrew Kennedy. "At least not for many years." But that would not bring back Noah, 7, John, 5, Paul, 3, Luke, 2, and Mary, 6 months.

TOO FAST
TO LIVE

Dale Earnhardt's shocking death could reform racing

Dale Earnhardt didn't figure to win the Daytona 500, but the view from fourth place going into the final lap looked fine. Ahead he could see his pal Michael Waltrip leading and his son Dale Jr. in second. Then, with less than a mile to go, Earnhardt's black No. 3 Chevrolet collided with another car and slammed head-on into a concrete wall. Only 49, he died instantly of head trauma, the fourth NASCAR fatality in just nine months at Daytona. Stunned fans made a pilgrimage to his North Carolina home to pay respects and to defend their hero's philosophy: "If you don't want to go fast, you shouldn't get in a race car." But sport officials questioned Earnhardt's decision, typical of his peers, not to wear proper head-and-neck support. While Dale Jr. also opposes

making such safety gear mandatory, he employed it in a race the following week and promptly wiped out, limping away without serious injury. Within five months, Junior, 26, went on to win the Pepsi 400 at the Daytona track where his father had died.

Earnhardt was bussed by third wife Teresa (left) at Daytona, three years before his fatal crash there (far right). His son (right) by second wife Brenda has said, "I know every time I get on the racetrack, I risk losing my life." Still, Junior stays in the sport, a tribute to his dad, NASCAR's dominant driver with 76 career wins.

Grabbing headlines in 2001 were a mole for Russia in the FBI, an unlikely alleged thief in the House of Windsor and a Hollywood wife whose murder remains unsolved. We also met a leader's love child, an ill-mannered Komodo dragon and an actress's other personality

herbal hopes

Suzanne Somers takes on cancer her own way

After a tabloid started snooping, Somers, 55, revealed that she had breast cancer. On *Larry King Live* she talked about her successful lumpectomy and radiation and her decision to turn down recommended chemotherapy in favor of Iscador, an alternative medicine made from mistletoe. But the ThighMaster-monger isn't pushing this alternative for everyone. "It's a huge burden for me that women might throw away their cancer drugs and go to Iscador," she said. "Because I don't know that it works. I'm hoping it does."

newsma

kers

royal moves

The Buck House bachelors venture onto new ground

It's a difficult day when you realize you must look up to talk to your sons. Prince Harry, 17, grazed 6 ft. in 2001, and Prince William, 19, had already hit 6'2". At a mere 5'10", Prince Charles, 53, could not deny his boys were growing up. At a summer polo match, Charles was thrown

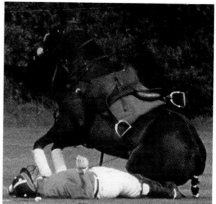

from his horse and lost consciousness for 30 seconds. He was fine but went to a hospital for observation. His sons played on, finishing victorious without him, perhaps bruising his ego even as they swelled it with pride. "Harry is at an age where he wants to prove himself," said polo commentator Jim Hilston. "You see good rivalry between father and son." There were other milestones. While carting William to St. Andrews University in a station wagon, Charles missed the entrance and had to back up, as Scottish onlookers lined the roads to glimpse the freshman. "I want to go there and be an ordinary student," said William, an art history major. It would be

hard with film crews around. Most agreed to let William alone, but one persisted. Turns out it worked for Charles's TV-producer brother Edward.

The year also marked the first time that William appeared at an event attended by his father's girlfriend, Camilla Parker Bowles, 54, who has her own room at two royal residences. "They get on with her quite well," said author Brian Hoey, "William perhaps slightly more than Harry." Added a family friend: They "want what is best for their father." Hoping to convince British subjects of the same, Charles and Camilla shared a first public kiss, at a London charity event. No Al and Tipper lip lock, the peck nonetheless appeared in every tabloid. No one would mistake Charles for a wild romantic, though many agree, said Hoey, "he's emerged as a very successful single parent."

an inside job?
A trusted butler is accused of theft

In life, she called him "my rock." Since Princess Diana's 1997 death, her closest aide, Paul Burrell, 43, had turned down book offers worth millions. Yet this least likely suspect was charged with stealing more than 300 of her personal items, including family letters and photos, a Valentino dress and the Indiana Jones bullwhip given by Harrison Ford. Last January Scotland Yard scoured the Cheshire home Burrell shares with his wife and two teenage sons. Later his brother Graham, 35, was also implicated, allegedly conspiring to sell the items, valued at $7 million. Both Burrells deny the charges. They are expected to stand trial in early 2002.

Before her accident, Taylor (left, with Gisele Bündchen in October) was the young face of Cover Girl. After (with James Renegar, inset), she said, "I sometimes feel like a 26-year-old in the body of an old woman."

driven to live

Six years after her sister's death, **Niki Taylor** survives a near-fatal car crash

Doctors told Barbara and Ken Taylor that they should think about possible funeral arrangements for their middle daughter, model Niki. Just six years earlier, their youngest, Krissy, also a model, died from asthma at 17. Now Niki, 26, lay in an Atlanta hospital with severe internal injuries suffered in a car accident in the early morning hours after a night of club-hopping. The driver of the car, Niki's friend James Renegar, 27, told police he was reaching for a cell phone when he lost control of his Nissan Maxima and smashed into a pole. There was no evidence that Renegar, who escaped without injury, had been drinking or otherwise under the influence. The third occupant of the car, friend John Lauck, 30, also walked away with barely a scratch.

For two months Taylor was near death. A vertebra was shattered, and her liver had been damaged—at one point it looked as if she would need a transplant. She would undergo 40 surgeries and suffer side effects such as a collapsed lung. Most painful for the divorced mother was not seeing her 6-year-old twin sons—children were not permitted in the intensive care unit. (Ex-husband Matt Martinez, 31, cared for the boys.) Miraculously, Taylor recovered sufficiently to fly home to Florida in July. A born-again Christian, she concluded, "I think the big man upstairs is saying, 'You've gotta live. It's not your time yet.'"

a shepherd

Jesse Jackson reveals his extramarital affair and child

During the Clinton-Lewinsky scandal, the Reverend Jesse Jackson acted as spiritual counsel to the President. But it turns out that Jackson, 60, was carrying on an extramarital affair of his own at the time and indeed had a daughter with Karin Stanford, 40, a political science profes-

sor who had run the D.C. office of his Rainbow/PUSH Coalition. Threat of exposure by the *National Enquirer* led Jackson to inform his wife of 38 years, Jackie, as well as the public. In a press statement, he admitted to fathering Ashley, now 2 (above, with Stanford, during an interview by Connie Chung). Jackson also conceded that he paid $3,000 monthly for child care and that he would take time away from his public ministry "to revive my spirit and reconnect with my family." Three days later he returned to his Chicago pulpit, explaining, "The ground is no place for a champion."

strays

but i play one on tv

I'm not a delinquent, insists Robert Iler

On *The Sopranos* he's no angel. A.J., the teen son of mobster Tony Soprano, has stolen exams and vandalized his school. But offscreen, actor Robert Iler, 16, seems the picture of a well-adjusted kid. He makes good grades and, said his admittedly biased mother, "is a good-hearted person." But in July Iler and two friends allegedly mugged two teens not far from the actor's New York City home, relieving them of $40. Surely he didn't need the money. Though his *Sopranos* earnings are put in a trust, Iler gets an ample allowance. In August he pleaded not guilty to charges of second-degree robbery and marijuana possession. While awaiting trial, Iler returned to school and the HBO set.

switching sides

Party-hopping Jim Jeffords turns a 50-50 Senate over to the Democrats

At any other time, the defection of Vermont Republican Jim Jeffords might have been only a minor loss to the GOP. After all, Jeffords, 67, often voted against his party, opposing the Reagan tax cut and favoring the Clintons' health-care reform. But in May, with the Senate deadlocked (and Vice President Dick Cheney breaking ties), Jeffords announced that he would become an independent "in order to best represent my state and my own conscience." Overnight, Tom Daschle replaced Trent Lott as majority leader and the Democrats held the reins. "He's always swimming against the tide," said Liz Daley, 62, who wed Jeffords in 1961, divorced him in '79 and has been remarried to him since '86.

role
reversal

Chelsea graduates, Hillary gets a job, and guess who's a political spouse?

It was the night before moving day, and the White House was filled with boxes marked "Library," "Chappaqua" and "Washington." The first group, to be unpacked at a presidential library in Arkansas, represented Bill Clinton's legacy, an issue of immediate concern as he closed his troubled tenure with a final scandal. That same night, he pardoned tax-evading fugitive Mark Rich and 139 others. (Brother-in-law Hugh Rodham had received $400,000 to lobby for two of the pardons but later returned the money.)

The second set of boxes was headed for suburban New York. Puttering around the house like Bob Vila, Clinton, 55, must be frustrated, figured Congressman Pete King, "to wake up in the morning, see a critical world problem on TV and not be able to try to resolve it." In July he settled clamorously in a Harlem office to work on the memoir he sold for $10 million ($2 mil more than Hillary's).

The last boxes went across D.C. to Hillary's home while Congress is in session. Pardongate gave her a rocky start, but the 54-year-old freshman proved herself. "She shows up having done her homework," cheered Senator Kent Conrad. Her husband helps out, vetting her speeches over the phone. Despite the long-distance relationship, the state of their union seemed strong. "They're just connected in some strange way," said a friend. They certainly were in June. Teary-eyed, they saw daughter Chelsea, 21, graduate from Stanford. Announcing she'd follow her dad's path to Oxford for a master's in history or international relations, this child of both a President and senator hinted at the burgeoning of a new political dynasty.

spy vs. spies
G-man Robert Hanssen turned mole for Russia

A 25-year veteran of the FBI's counterintelligence unit, Hanssen, 57, seemed an unlikely mole. He lived in a Virginia suburb with his wife, six kids and dog. On Sundays he attended mass with FBI director Louis Freeh. But since 1985 he had spied for Russia in exchange for $1 million in cash and diamonds. Worst of all, he fingered U.S. agents in Moscow who were later executed.

Nabbed during a drop near his home, Hanssen was convicted and awaits sentencing. The FBI was embarrassed by its obliviousness, but others were also fooled. "He has always been very honest," said his mother, Vivian, 88. "I don't understand how he could be leading a double life."

ruth, maris, mcgwire...
...and now Barry Bonds

Babe Ruth's season record of 60 home runs in 1927 lasted until Roger Maris's 61 in 1961. Thirty-seven years later, Mark McGwire smacked 70, only to be bested three years later by San Francisco Giant Barry Bonds, 37. Suffering from a surly image earlier in his career, Bonds seemed to mellow slightly, culminating with his 73rd homer in his last game of 2001. The son of all-star Bobby Bonds and godson of Hall of Famer Willie Mays, Bonds was greeted at the plate that day by his own son, bat boy Nikolai, 11.

unso
mystery

Who murdered Robert Blake's troubled wife?

On a May evening, Robert Blake and wife Bonny Lee Bakley shared a meal at a favorite Italian eatery near their Los Angeles home. After leaving the restaurant together, Blake, 67, says he ran back to retrieve a gun he'd left at the table. (He carried the licensed weapon at his wife's insistence; she said she was being stalked.) When he returned to the car, he found her shot in the head, struggling to breathe. She died shortly after. At Bakley's graveside, Blake spoke like a man in grief over the loss of his bride of less than a year. "I will do everything I can to make our daughter Rosie's life the best I can," he vowed. "I promise you that, Bonny."

But the relationship between the *Baretta* actor and his wife was more complicated than his public mourning suggested. Starstruck, Bakley, 44, had often told friends her goal was to snare a famous mate. After pursuing Jerry Lee Lewis for 10 years, she finally landed Blake in 1999. Marrying only after DNA tests proved that Rose, 1, was in fact his child (it was thought that Marlon Brando's son Christian might be the father), the couple lived in separate bungalows on Blake's property. And before wedding Bakley, a convicted con artist who ran date-by-mail scams, he asked her to sign a prenup, agreeing not to conduct business from home or consort with known felons in the presence of their daughter.

While Blake's lawyer circulated negative stories about Bakley and suggested that the perpetrator may have been a shady character from her past, police searched the actor's home. By late fall, Blake had been neither named nor ruled out as a suspect. Still, he was forced to sell his home, which had become a stop, along with O.J. Simpson's house and the site of the Manson murders, on a grisly bus tour. Said Bakley friend Linda Gail Lewis: "I hope wherever Bonny is, she can see all this. This is what she always wanted: to be the center of attention."

ved

Bakley (inset) had two grown children from a first marriage and another she claimed was fathered by Jerry Lee Lewis. Blake, said his lawyer, "married her because she was the mother of his daughter."

what kind of tree, celestia?

Anne Heche introduces her spacey alter ego to Barbara Walters

Besides the talk of spaceships, it was a classic Walters weepy. On *20/20* to promote her book *Call Me Crazy,* Anne Heche poured forth with stories of talking with God (not in prayer but actual dialogue) and hearing voices that told her—or her other personality, Celestia—to take Ecstasy and board a shuttle to another dimension. She spoke fondly of her three-year relationship with Ellen DeGeneres but added

During their ABC taping, Heche (left) and Walters toured various locations, including a New York City flea market.

pioneer spirit
Geraldine Ferraro fights cancer

In 1984 veep candidate Ferraro became the first woman on a major presidential ticket. She and Walter Mondale lost but "took down the Men Only sign at the White House," said Ferraro. In June she revealed that she was facing a far greater challenge. In 1998 Ferraro, 66, and husband John Zaccaro, 68, learned she had multiple myeloma, a bone-marrow cancer usually fatal within five years. Again she's at the forefront, undergoing experimental treatment, including thalidomide, which may have pushed the disease into remission. Said her friend Senator Barbara Mikulski: "She's approaching this with the same grit and spirit and humor that she pursues politics."

that she was "insane" at the time and concluded that her delusions were a coping mechanism to deal with her memories of being molested by her late father. (Heche's mother and sister dispute her allegations.) All this, said Heche, explained why she had been found wandering into a stranger's home in Fresno, California. But within a year, Heche, 32, pronounced herself sane and ready for the Walters confessional. Subsequently married (see page 73) and pregnant with a baby due in 2002, Heche concluded, reassuringly, "I'm here, and I could not be more elated with my life."

there's always a loophole . . .
A *Rules* girl gets divorced

As *The Rules: Time-Tested Secrets for Capturing the Heart of Mr. Right* tore up bestseller lists in 1995, it also drew jeers from feminists and other skeptics. Ellen Fein (far right, with coauthor Sherrie Schneider) deflected criticism by pointing to her long marriage to pharmacist Paul Feingertz, with whom she has two kids. But just before the book's second sequel, *The Rules for Marriage: Time-Tested Secrets for Making Your Marriage Work*, hit stores, news broke that Fein, 43, was splitting after 16 years. Her fame, she said, was a factor, adding, "I still 100 percent believe in *The Rules*."

couple of close calls

Sharon Stone has a scare, and her hubby tangles with a dragon

As a Father's Day gift for her husband, *San Francisco Chronicle* executive editor Phil Bronstein, 50, Sharon Stone arranged a private tour of the Los Angeles Zoo. (The couple have a 1-year-old son, Roan.) The visit climaxed with an invitation to pet Komo, the zoo's Komodo dragon. Warned that Komo might mistake his white sneakers for tasty white rats, Bronstein took off his shoes. "So Phil gets in the cage," Stone recalls, "and I took a picture. As he started to move, this thing just lunged at him." Refusing to panic, the editor pried open the jaws of the 7-ft. Indonesian lizard and extracted his foot. By then his big toe was crushed and a few tendons were torn, hospitalizing him for five days. "He has an un-

believable calm under pressure," said Stone.

That calm was further tested a few months later, when his 43-year-old wife suffered an unexplained brain hemorrhage, probably the result of an aneurysm. Stone checked into a San Francisco neurological facility, but doctors found no permanent brain damage. For two weeks Stone remained under watch for complications (none were reported) of what she dubbed "the mysteries."

our air apparent

Retired twice, Michael Jordan returns to play Wizard of Aahs

"If Michael wants to come back, God bless him," said Kobe Bryant, who reigned with Allen Iverson and Vince Carter as stars of the post-Jordan era. Turns out that era lasted only three seasons before Jordan gave up part-ownership of the Washington Wizards to don their jersey. Fans wondered why Jordan, at 38, would risk tarnishing the NBA's most lustrous legend. Certainly not for the money. (He is donating his $1 million token salary to victims of the September 11 Disaster Relief Fund.) His simple explanation: "I am returning as a player to the game I love."

show
of shows

A Broadway baby at 75, Mel Brooks learns once again why it's good to be the king

More than 30 years ago, Mel Brooks stood triumphant at the podium, clutching his Best Screenplay Oscar for *The Producers*. "I must tell you what's in my heart," he recalls saying. "Ba-bump. Ba-bump. Ba-bump." Flash forward to the 2001 Tony Awards, where his heart was likely doing an extended drum solo as the musical stage version of his 1968 film collected a record 12 honors. Prodded by actress wife Anne Bancroft, Brooks had written music and lyrics to retell the story of a lovably sleazy Broadway producer, Max Bialystock (Zero Mostel in the film), and his pushover accountant, Leo Bloom (Gene Wilder back then). The pair bilk investors by selling far more than 100 percent of a show titled *Springtime for Hitler.* It is sure to be a flop, they reason, allowing them to abscond with the money. Then *Springtime* becomes an unlikely smash.

A Broadway novice, Brooks enlisted the director-choreographer of the moment Susan Stroman (*Contact*), and angels (as stage backers are known) fought for the chance to put their money behind *The Producers.* Never mind that this would be Broadway's first comedy to feature goose-stepping chorus lines, a Busby Berkeleyesque showstopper of gray-haired ladies tapping their walkers in rhythm, and couplets like "Don't be stupid, be a smarty/ Come and join the Nazi party." With the promise of Nathan Lane creating the musical mutation of the producer and Matthew Broderick sliding into the bookkeeper's green visor and soft shoes, theatergoers snapped up $13 million in advance sales of New York's priciest ticket: $100 each. After the first reviews were published, box offices of other shows were enlisted to handle the rush. By November the best seats went for $480 apiece. Though Brooks hadn't created a well-received film in years, he was suddenly in demand. Still, he felt more like the sheepish Bloom than the boisterous Bialystock. "That's me: a little kid from Brooklyn who finally made it across the vast East River to Broadway. That's a journey that is as great as the Alleghenies to the Rockies."

HOT
PROPERTIES

Out with the old and in with the new: Fame's freshman class of 2001 included child star and Harry Potter personifier Daniel Radcliffe, musical find and Britney alternative Alicia Keys, prime-time séance master John Edward

moonlighting in the morning

Live host Kelly Ripa keeps her other day job

How to tell Regis Philbin's new perky host from his old one? Unlike her predecessor, said TV authority Robert Thompson, Ripa "doesn't seem like she is taking dictation from Neptune." After 11 years on *All My Children*, Ripa, 31, filled the chair vacated by Kathie Lee Gifford. A Jersey girl married to her soap costar Mark Consuelos, also 31, Ripa gave birth to their second child shortly after joining Reege. The rigors of doing double duty aside, she's pleased by the new challenge. "My *All My Children* character is a recovering alcoholic with split personality," she notes. "After all these years, it will be wonderful to play myself."

The Quiz Mistress

Called the rudest woman on TV, *Weakest Link* host Anne Robinson scores as the anti-Reege

Just as viewers began to tire of quoting "Is that your final answer?" NBC made a new bid for most annoyingly memorable game show catchphrase. "You *are* the weakest link. Goodbye!" Delivered with an English schoolmarm's disapproval, the line sprang from the mind of Anne Robinson, who hosts both the British and new American versions of *Weakest Link*. Her dismissive trademark is a tribute to an aunt who used to shoo people out of her room with a pointed "Goodbye." Robinson, 57, had been directed in the original BBC version to coddle disappointed contestants as their peers voted them off the show, ending their chances of winning up to $30,000. But she soon found that tough love—"Is there no *beginning* to your intelligence?" she asked one player—made her more popular than playing a softy.

Born in Liverpool, Robinson was formerly a Fleet Street journalist and TV consumer advocate. Once Britain's highest-paid newswoman, she is now reportedly raking in more than $4 million a year as a transcontinental host. Divorced, remarried and the mother of one, she relishes her new role as quiz show sadist. (Surely she is the first: Could Wink Martindale pull off wearing that black leather duster? Pat Sajak?) But her family argues that it's all an act. "She's more dungarees than dominatrix," says daughter Emma, a radio talk show host in Washington, D.C. As if to signal viewers that her taunts are all in good fun, Robinson ends each *Link* episode with a wink to the camera. And behind the scenes she insists, "I'm not evil incarnate."

oprah's reality check

Like it or not, TV shrink Dr. Phil tells it like it is

Years ago a couple came to psychotherapist Phil McGraw for help. Within 10 minutes he blurted, "No wonder you people don't like each other. I can't stand either one of you!" After a decade in the field, he focused more on being a trial consultant. In 1997 he was hired to aid Oprah Winfrey's defense in a libel suit brought by the beef industry. Winfrey won, and she and McGraw, 51, became close friends. Soon he was a steady guest on her show. Now he commutes weekly from the Dallas home he shares with wife Robin, two sons and a beagle named Cozmo in order to dispense his frank advice. "Get real" is a favorite admonition. He has no patience with whiners, mommy blamers or anyone who uses the word "codependent." His adages have sent two books, including the wildly popular *Life Strategies,* to the bestseller list. Surprised by his fame and by the fans who shout "Dr. Phil!" when they spot him, McGraw marvels at "the power of Oprah's platform." Indeed. This summer he will premiere his own show, a creation of Winfrey's Harpo Productions.

the survivor

Pearl Harbor behind him, **Josh Hartnett** rebounds

"The guy will have beautiful women camped out on his front lawn for months," predicted costar Ben Affleck just before *Pearl Harbor* came out. While the movie didn't do for Hartnett what *Titanic* did for Leonardo DiCaprio, it did prove that the 23-year-old Minnesotan could survive appearing in an overhyped critical turkey. Soon after, his turn as a teen Iago in *O* earned Hartnett warm reviews and his share of female fans. *Harbor* producer Jerry Bruckheimer bet on him again for the winter release *Black Hawk Down*, the story of the doomed U.S. mission in Somalia. "He's a throwback to old Hollywood," raved Bruckheimer. "The sensitivity of Montgomery Clift and the honesty and dignity of Gary Cooper." As for his own stardom, the single Hartnett says, "I'm going to ride this as long as I can. Fame is temporary, so sooner or later the plane is gonna land."

blue streak

Ichiro Suzuki is a hit

Seattle tourism ads used to lure Japanese travelers with images of the Space Needle or Mt. Rainier
a new local hero originally from Kasugai. More and more visiting fans at the Mariners' stadium wave Rising Sun flags and posters written in kanji. "In Japan," said a Mariner exec, "he's a rock star." Which isn't to say that Seattle hasn't warmed to the right fielder his teammates call Wizard. What's not to like about a rookie (with nine Japanese seasons under his belt) who topped the American League in batting (.350) and hits (242) and led the Mariners to the League Championship Series? The Mariners paid the Orix Blue Wave $13 million to release Suzuki, who got $14 million for three years and relocated with his wife, Yumiko. He is the only player in the majors with his first name on his uniform, but Suzuki, 28, is trying to blend in. He learned from teammate Ryan Franklin to say "Chillin' like Bob Dylan." "Then," Franklin adds, "I had to teach him who Bob Dylan is."

scaling the charts

Singer-pianist Alicia Keys does it her way

"Everyone asks how it feels to have your album be No. 1. It feels great. But the important thing is that it's really *my* music out there," said Alicia Keys, 20, of her debut, *Songs in A Minor.* Four years ago producers saw her as the next teen-pop thing. But Keys (born Alicia Cook in New York City), who played piano at 7 and composed as a teen, had her own sound in mind—an eclectic mix of classical, R&B and hip-hop. She bravely wriggled out of her original contract and got rediscovered by Clive Davis, who had launched Whitney Houston and Janis Joplin. Critics predict that Keys could become similarly iconic. For now she is savoring her stellar debut. It is, she said, "a priceless moment. Like your first kiss, it never happens again."

a long way from lucy

Ashley Martin gives football a kick in the pants

Besides Lucy from *Peanuts,* name one female football player. Hard to do, right? So it was big news when Ashley Martin, a 20-year-old junior at Alabama's Jacksonville State, took the field in August. Martin herself felt she was there not to make points but to score them. "I'm not trying to break a barrier," said the 5'11" backup kicker. "I just want to play a game and help the team win." She did, with three extra points, becoming the first woman to score in an NCAA football game. Though at college on a soccer scholarship, Martin had played football in high school in Sharpsburg, Georgia, where she accepted the homecoming queen crown in her uniform and cleats. Jacksonville State football coach Jack Crowe recruited Martin after watching her kicking soccer balls from his window. Soon her male teammates accepted her. Said offensive lineman Jeremy Sullivan: "It was kind of funny to see a ponytail sticking out of a helmet. But after a while it was like, 'That's just another kicker.' "

laugh track
TV improv master Wayne Brady gets his own gig

"I hope you can bring us back," variety-show veteran Carol Burnett told Brady, who is attempting to resurrect the format. Widely known as the fastest, and often funniest, improviser on the ad-libbed *Whose Line Is It Anyway?*, Brady earned an ABC series of his own that rivals *Line* in laughs per minute. On *The Wayne Brady Show,* the star is joined by a troupe of sketch comics and musicians, who complement his talent for absurd humor (in one scene his James Brown becomes a soul-singing paramedic) and for impersonation (Michael Jackson is unlikely to be a fan). Raised by his paternal grandmother in Orlando, Brady, 29, got his start playing Tigger and Goofy at Walt Disney World and later hit the dinner-theater circuit. He landed *Line* after a six-hour audition in 1998. Married to dancer Mandie Brady, 25, he is savoring his good fortune, including an Emmy nomination. The only trouble? "Now the whole world," says Brady, "knows what a geek I am."

author! author!

The Corrections' **Jonathan Franzen** proves his audacity

Novelist Franzen created a literary fuss with a 1996 *Harper's* essay in which he posited that big, serious social fiction was being killed off by the TV age, then took a vow to single-handedly resuscitate the form. Franzen, 42 and divorced, holed up in New York City and wrote while wearing earplugs and a blindfold to shut out everything but his fictional world. His setting was the Midwest (he's from St. Louis), and the resulting novel, *The Corrections*, was a spellbinding, hilarious saga of family dysfunction. Highbrow reviewers swooned over him ("A wizard," said *The Atlantic Monthly*), and Oprah Winfrey pumped up the print order by picking it for her book club. But after he indicated ambivalence about having her logo on his work, Winfrey canceled her televised dinner with Franzen, a custom for her anointed authors. "We're moving on to the next book," said the host. So, presumably, is Franzen.

good clean fun

SpongeBob SquarePants soaks up the love

Marine-biologist-turned-animator Stephen Hillenberg noticed something few people had: a dearth of phylum Porifera on TV. In other words, said Hillenberg, 39, "there's never been a main character that was a sponge." He filled that void by pitching Nickelodeon an idea for a cartoon series. (Hillenberg, who used to guide tide-pool field trips, carted a small aquarium to the meeting.) Two years later his *SpongeBob SquarePants* is closing in on *Rugrats* as the most-watched kids' program. An ageless, guileless boy-man (think Pee-wee Herman, but porous), SpongeBob (with pet snail Gary, who meows like a cat and writes Beat poetry) lives in a pineapple duplex in the undersea town of Bikini Bottom. His best friend is a flaky starfish named Patrick, and his main squeeze is the sponge-worthy Sandy Cheeks, a surfer-girl squirrel. He toils days making Krabby Patties at the Krusty Krab diner, alongside a squid called Squidward Tentacles, who plays the clarinet and dabbles in interpretive dance. The quirky cast charmed not only kids but also adults, including Sigourney Weaver and Dr. Dre. Cheers Rob Lowe: "You have to love a sponge in tightie-whities."

dialing the dead zone

Psychic John Edward syndicates his sixth sense

Only 15 when a psychic indicated that he might be similarly gifted, Long Islander John Edward dabbled in phlebotomy (drawing blood in a lab) and ballroom-dance instruction before unleashing his supernatural talents. First he did private readings, purporting to connect clients with the dead. Then he took calls on the radio. In 2001 his TV show *Crossing Over with John Edward* became its own unexplained phenomenon. Skeptics say he's employing a trick called "cold reading," merely throwing out generalities ("I'm hearing a mother figure . . .") and filling in details by picking up cues from the audience member whose late mum is allegedly on the line. If he strikes out, those readings can be edited out before the show tape airs. Edward's only problem is his growing fame. "It's hard when somebody stops you in a restaurant," he says. "You're trying to have your own private time, and they're going, 'Is my mom standing behind me?'"

sharing the wealth

A solo success, Nelly returns to his group roots

Rapping with the St. Lunatics since 1993, Nelly (born Cornell Haynes Jr. in St. Louis) broke out after he was offered a solo recording deal. The band gave him a sabbatical, assuming it would open the door for all of them. "We knew he could get the young girls who buy a lot of records," said St. Lunatic Ali Jones. "He had the face, the six-pack abs and that melodic vocal style." They were right. Nelly scored a platinum album with *Country Grammar,* named for a black dialect. That led to a film role in *Snipes,* a spot onstage with Aerosmith at the Super Bowl halftime show and a "Nelly Day" at Busch Stadium to honor the onetime pro baseball prospect. By then he was ready to introduce the St. Lunatics to his legions of fans. Their ensemble effort *Free City* flew off the racks. "It's hectic, man," said Nelly, 23. "I just shot a movie, filmed a video, recorded an album. My feet hurt!"

off to be the wizard

The envy of his Harry Potter-crazed pals, actor Daniel Radcliffe goes to the top of the class at Hogwarts School

J.K. Rowling's *Harry Potter* books are loved by some 100 million readers. Until recently Daniel Radcliffe was not among them. He read two, then tired of the series—and of most books, which paled, in his opinion, next to wrestling. So his London schoolmates, *Potter* fans all, can be forgiven for being, in Radcliffe's words, "a bit angry" upon hearing he had won the role of the student wizard in the film. Radcliffe's parents, Alan, a literary agent, and Marcia Gresham, a casting director, were initially against having him anchor the most anticipated kiddie-lit adaptation since *The Wizard of Oz*. Director Chris Columbus was sympathetic. "I felt a need to protect these kids against . . . what can go wrong if you star in a film of this magnitude," said Columbus, who had launched Macaulay Culkin's career in *Home Alone*. Despite Radcliffe's short résumé (listing only the BBC's *David Copperfield* and a small role in *The Tailor of Panama*), he possessed a maturity that gave the filmmaker faith. "Dan is an 11-year-old with a 35-year-old heart."

mile

jennifer lopez & cris judd

Playing an onscreen wedding planner may have given Lopez, 32, inspiration for her own nuptials. Only four months after choreographer Judd, also 32, proposed, the pair walked down a rose-petal-strewn aisle on a mountain-top in Calabasas, California. Her high-profile romance with Sean Combs seemed eons away (though it had ended just the previous February). This night, said *Wedding Planner* director Adam Shankman, "was not about her being J.Lo. It was about her becoming Mrs. Cris Judd."

First came love, then came marriage for Jennifer Lopez and her dancer beau; and Angie Harmon found her Prince Charming in Giants clothing. Celine Dion and husband René Angélil plus single mom Camryn Manheim were pushing baby carriages. And, sadly, Ted & Jane and Kim & Alec reached the end of the road

stones

weddings HERE COME THE BRIDES...

OTHER NUPTIALS: ACTORS **Jennie Garth** & **Peter Facinelli** ON JAN. 20 ● N.Y. YANKEE **David Justice** & MODEL **Rebecca Villalobos** ON FEB. 8 ● MUSICIAN **James Taylor** & SYMPHONY EXEC **Caroline Smedvig** ON FEB. 18 ● INDIANAPOLIS COLT **Peyton Manning** & MARKETER **Ashley Thompson** ON MAR. 17 ● L.A. LAKER **Kobe Bryant** & **Vanessa Laine** ON APRIL 18 ● BLINK-182's **Tom DeLonge** & DESIGNER **Jennifer Jenkins** ON MAY 26 ● ROCKER **Tom Petty** & **Dana York** ON JUNE 3 ● ACTORS **Jason Bateman** & **Amanda Anka** ON JULY 3 ● ACTRESS **Jennifer Grey** & SCREENWRITER **Clark Gregg** ON JULY 21 ● EURYTHMIC **Dave Stewart** & PHOTOGRAPHER **Anoushka Fisz** ON AUG. 4 ● ACTRESS **Geena Davis** & SURGEON **Reza Jarrahy** ON SEPT. 1 ● COUNTRY SINGERS **Lorrie Morgan** & **Sammy Kershaw** ON SEPT. 29 ● ACTORS **Harvey Keitel** & **Daphna Kastner** ON OCT. 8

pierce brosnan & keely shaye smith

Friends wondered if the wedding of Brosnan, 49, and his seven-year girl-friend would ever take place. A May 2000 plan was nixed after Brosnan's son Sean was in a car wreck. Another date was lost when Smith, 37, became pregnant. Finally, on August 4, guests gathered in Ireland. The ceremony was delayed 20 minutes, however, while Smith nursed 5-month-old Paris.

lauren holly
& francis greco

▼ Her marriage to Danny Quinn, son of actor Anthony, lasted only three years, her union with Jim Carrey only 10 months. But Holly, 37, never gave up on love. In January she announced her engagement to Greco, 32, a New York City investment banker. Two months later, on March 10, the pair wed at Holy Rosary Church in Toronto, the groom's (and Carrey's) hometown. Said Father Paul McGill: "They're a wonderful couple and they seem faithful and sincere."

natalie cole &
kenneth dupree

▲ In the Nashville Baptist church of which he is the pastor, Dupree, 45, became the third husband of singer Cole, 51, on October 13. Guests included Dionne Warwick and Cole's *Unforgettable* producer, David Foster. The ceremony was "spiritual and sacred," said wedding coordinator Jayne Bubis. "It was just like Natalie—elegant."

tommy lee jones & dawn maria laurel

▼ Of Jones's second marriage, to Kimberlea Cloughley, with whom he had two children, a friend said, "It was like *Green Acres*: He likes the country, she likes the city." Six years after the split, Jones, 54, wed photographer Laurel, 36, near his Texas home on March 19. Auspiciously, he's interested in photography, and both enjoy polo.

christina applegate & johnathon schaech

▲ Even 10 years of playing the daughter on TV's take on highly dysfunctional family life, *Married . . . with Children,* didn't dissuade Applegate, 29, from heading down that path herself. On October 20, with her *Married* costars Katey Sagal and David Faustino among the 130 celebrants, Applegate wed actor Schaech, 32, in Palm Springs. The couple exchanged rings and red roses before Catholic and United Church of Religious Science clergy. "There was no question," observed one guest, "how much they love each other."

brooke shields & chris henchy

Shields and TV producer Henchy's first wedding on April 4 was a small civil proceeding on California's Catalina Island. Recalling the chaos at her 1997 marriage to Andre Agassi, Shields, 35, thought that those decoy nuptials to Henchy, 37, would throw the press off. Sated, few reporters knew about the second wedding on May 26, a Catholic ceremony attended by family and friends at a private Palm Beach estate. The ruse worked. Said the bride: "It was absolutely perfect."

drew barrymore & tom green

▼ They almost followed Tiny Tim into history by getting hitched on late-night TV. But at the last minute Barrymore, 26, vetoed the idea of marrying on *Saturday Night Live* in 2000. Though rumors persisted that they had eloped in March 2001, she and comic actor Green, 29, didn't make it official until July 7 with a Malibu wedding. To the strains of "Ave Maria," the bride, escorted by her mother, Jaid, wore a cream gown; the groom, a tuxedo. Then there were the lyric sheets, passed out to guests, for a song about drag racing—apropos of nothing, save for the couple's shared sense of humor.

suzanne pleshette & tom poston

▲ Four decades after they first met, the two Bob Newhart costars became husband and wife. Pleshette, 64, played Newhart's wife on his first series, while Poston, 79, was the handyman on the second. Each married other people, and each was recently widowed. Wed on May 11, the pair, said matchmaker Newhart, "are like teenagers. It's too bad they don't have rumble seats so they can make out."

anne heche & coleman laffoon

Until their August 2000 split, Heche, 32, and Ellen DeGeneres called each other "wife" and wore gold bands. On September 1, 2001, the actress wed Laffoon, 27, a cameraman she met shooting a documentary about DeGeneres. Heche was in Badgley Mischka, Laffoon in a fur-trimmed Valentino. "I'm in a straight relationship," said Heche (who had previously dated guys, including Steve Martin). "That doesn't mean I call myself straight."

angie harmon & jason sehorn

Some 400 guests—actors, athletes and Texas society ladies among them—came to cheer the June 9 Dallas marriage of actress Harmon, 28, and New York Giants cornerback Sehorn, 30. The couple planned to set up house nearby, in Harmon's hometown. "You've got to live where your heart is," said Sehorn. "My heart is wherever Angie is."

toni braxton & keri lewis

The once-bankrupt R&B singer happily bore a $75,000 ring and a $15,000 Vera Wang gown. The cake was designed to look like a stack of blue Tiffany boxes. Her money problems obviously in the past, Braxton, 34, had a lot to celebrate on April 21, when she married musician Lewis, 30, in a wisteria-and-rose-filled Atlanta garden.

babies
LITTLE THINGS MEAN A LOT...

ALSO BORN: TO ACTRESS **Jane Leeves** & TV EXEC **Marshall Coben,** DAUGHTER **Isabella,** JAN. 9 • TO SINGER **Marc Anthony** & FORMER MISS UNIVERSE **Dayanara Torres,** SON **Cristian,** FEB. 5 • TO SINGERS **Vince Gill** & **Amy Grant,** DAUGHTER **Corrina,** MAR. 12 • TO DIXIE CHICK **Natalie Maines** & ACTOR **Adrian Pasdar,** SON **Jackson,** MAR. 15 • TO SINGER **Clint Black** & ACTRESS **Lisa Hartman Black,** DAUGHTER **Lily,** MAY 8 • TO ACTORS **Lisa Rinna** & **Harry Hamlin,** DAUGHTER **Amelia,** JUNE 13 • TO MUSICIAN **Eric Clapton** & ARTIST **Melia McEnery,** DAUGHTER **Julie,** JUNE 13 • TO ACTORS **Kirk Cameron** & **Chelsea Noble,** DAUGHTER **Olivia,** JULY 18 • TO ACTORS **Tisha Campbell** & **Duane Martin,** SON **Xen,** AUG. 8 • TO ACTRESS **Laura Dern** & MUSICIAN **Ben Harper,** SON **Ellery,** AUG. 21 • TO ACTRESS **Jodie Foster,** SON **Kit,** SEPT. 29 • TO ACTOR **Kelsey Grammer** & WIFE **Camille,** DAUGHTER **Mason,** OCT. 24 • TO ACTORS **Michael J. Fox** & **Tracy Pollan,** DAUGHTER **Esme,** NOV. 5

kevin sorbo & sam jenkins

After two years of trying to conceive, the former *Hercules* star and his actress wife were considering adoption. Then Jenkins, 36, discovered she was pregnant. "The stress," speculates Sorbo, 42, "kept us from succeeding." August 22 saw the arrival of a boy, Braeden, at a hospital near their Las Vegas home. "It was," said Sorbo, "instantaneous and unconditional love."

cindy crawford & rande gerber

"I want a big family," said Crawford, 35, after the 1999 birth of her first child, son Presley. She and husband Gerber, 39, a restaurateur, took another step toward that goal on September 3, when the model gave birth at home in Los Angeles (reportedly without painkillers) to a daughter, Kaia. Married for three years, Crawford said that having kids "made our relationship much stronger. Watching your husband become a father is really sexy and wonderful."

celine dion & rené angélil

Known in the French-Canadian press as *le petit prince,* tiny René-Charles, born January 25 in Florida, was his parents' reward after a long and frustrating course of fertility treatments. Though Dion, 32, and her manager husband Angélil, 59, agreed to put her recording career on hold for at least a year in order to become parents, "this baby will be sung to constantly," predicts her brother Michel. "Celine is always singing. She can't help it."

andre agassi & steffi graf

Four days after his parents wed in a stealth ceremony in Las Vegas, Jaden Agassi arrived October 26. The boy's mother, 32, retired from tennis with 22 Grand Slam titles; his father, 31, has won 7. The Berlin papers, which follow his German-born mom's every move, are calling him "super baby." That may be also because they don't get his Americanized moniker. One headline demanded, "Steffi, what kind of strange name is that?"

camryn manheim

▼ Son Milo Jacob became the man in her life when the single actress gave birth on March 6. Declining to name the father, Manheim, 40, said only, "It's not David Crosby."

calista flockhart

▲ The *Ally McBeal* star rang in the new year in a San Diego maternity ward, watching the birth of Liam, the son she would adopt. Thrilled to be a first-time mom, Flockhart, 36, has said that a romantic relationship is "not a priority."

kim basinger
& alec baldwin

A neighbor in Long Island's Hamptons, Monte Farber, saw the couple dancing in July 2000 and believed "they would have stayed together forever." Family knew better. After the actress, 47, filed for divorce in January, her father, Don, said, "I've known for a year and a half that she was thinking about this." What apparently moved her to end their seven-year marriage was Baldwin's untamed temper tantrums, particularly in front of their daughter Ireland, 5. While insiders concede that Baldwin, 42, angers easily, one of them added that Basinger "is not exactly a poster girl for stability." The still-friendly couple, seen out together post-split, planned to share custody of Ireland.

divorces SOME SAID IT WOULDN'T LAST... AND IT DIDN'T

OTHER SPLITS: ACTOR **Robert Downey Jr.** & SINGER **Deborah Falconer** (AFTER 8 YEARS) • *SURVIVOR* HOST **Jeff Probst** & PSYCHOTHERAPIST **Shelley Wright** (5 YEARS) • VOLLEYBALL PRO **Gabrielle Reece** & SURFER **Laird Hamilton** (3 YEARS) • ACTOR **Gary Oldman** & PHOTOGRAPHER **Donya Fiorentino** (4 YEARS) • DIRECTOR **Robert Townsend** & REAL ESTATE AGENT **Cheri Townsend** (10 YEARS) • MÖTLEY CRÜE BASSIST **Nikki Sixx** & ACTRESS **Donna D'Errico** (4 YEARS) • NEW YORK CITY MAYOR **Rudy Giuliani** & TV PERSONALITY **Donna Hanover** (17 YEARS) • DIRECTOR **Peter Bogdanovich** & ACTRESS **Louise Hoogstraten** (12 YEARS) • MODEL **Cheryl Tiegs** & YOGA INSTRUCTOR **Rod Stryker** (3 YEARS)

janet jackson & rené elizondo jr.

Even her own father never knew they were married. ("He can't keep a secret," said Jackson, 35.) If their marriage hadn't ended, *we* might never have known it existed. But over the summer word leaked that they had, in fact, wed a decade before and that Elizondo, 38, was suing Jackson to break their prenup agreement, claiming that his influence over her music and marketing entitled him to a greater slice—up to $25 million—of her fortune. Indeed, before the split, according to Jackson, the couple had never been apart for more than a week. Then, while traveling solo on tour, she mused, "Funny how things change."

kate winslet &
jim threapleton

▼ The *Titanic* star, who met her director husband in 1997 on the set of *Hideous Kinky,* had talked about their marriage as having "highs and lows," and she added, "At times it's tough." By September, Winslet, 25, and Threapleton, 27, called it quits. The couple have a year-old daughter, Mia.

jane fonda
& ted turner

▲ "My favorite ex-husband is here," said Fonda, 63, when Turner, 62, showed up with a new girlfriend at an Atlanta charity auction Fonda was hosting. Just months after filing for divorce (the third for both)—Fonda's new devotion to Christianity reportedly played a part—the pair were able to share a joke. When a trip to Fonda's New Mexico ranch went on the block, Turner bid $12,000 and won.

jack & kristina wagner

▼ They met on the *General Hospital* set in 1984 but "didn't start seriously dating until I got pregnant [in 1990]," said Kristina, 38, of her romance with costar Jack Wagner, 41. "Well, maybe a couple of months before." Married in 1993, they had two sons before splitting in February.

marion jones & c.j. hunter

▲ Married for only three years—less than the time between Summer Olympics—Jones, the star of the 2000 Games with five track-and-field medals, and Hunter, a world shot-put champion, made their split public in June, citing irreconcilable differences. He had tested positive for drugs during her moment of glory in Sydney. Jones, 25, would say only that her difficulty with Hunter, 32, was "a distraction. It will be good to have it done with."

harrison ford & melissa mathison

Ford, 59, once conceded, "I'm probably a better actor than I am a father or husband." In 2001, after a brief split and reconciliation, screenwriter Mathison, 51, his wife of 18 years, filed for legal separation and asked for joint custody of their kids, Malcolm, 14, and Georgia, 11. One Jackson Hole, Wyoming, neighbor speculated that Ford's "moodiness and reclusiveness" may have been a factor. "Many women might have left him a long time ago."

eminem & kim mathers

▼ Did it surprise anyone that the Detroit rapper who wrote songs about killing his wife ended up in court with her? After a tumultuous 2½-year marriage, Eminem, 29, and Mathers, 26, finally ended it amicably, agreeing to share custody of their daughter Hailie Jade, 6.

courtney thorne-smith & andrew conrad

▲ Theirs may be Hollywood's easiest divorce, as the actress and her geneticist beau might never have been legally hitched. After their first date four years ago, Thorne-Smith, 34, and Conrad, 38, celebrated in 2000 with an impromptu Hawaiian wedding—but no sign of a marriage license. Seven months after taking their vows they split, even as Thorne-Smith graced the cover of a magazine in her bridal gown.

'I love the world! I'm so happy!' beamed Julia Roberts at the Oscars. Winners echoed her sentiments at the Grammys and other shows early in the year. But then life changed, the Emmys were delayed, and show folk looked forward to the day when they could again roll out the red carpet

hollywood's

"I should have bet on myself," said surprised winner Marcia Gay Harden (second from left), who shared acting honors with Benicio Del Toro, Julia Roberts and Russell Crowe.

big nights

the oscars

THE ENVELOPES, PLEASE . . .

BEST PICTURE: *Gladiator* • BEST
DIRECTOR: **Steven Soderbergh,** *Traffic*
• BEST ACTRESS: **Julia Roberts,** *Erin Brockovich* • BEST ACTOR: **Russell Crowe,** *Gladiator* • BEST SUPPORTING ACTRESS: **Marcia Gay Harden,** *Pollock* • BEST SUPPORTING ACTOR: **Benicio Del Toro,** *Traffic* • BEST ORIGINAL SCREENPLAY: **Cameron Crowe,** *Almost Famous* • BEST ADAPTED SCREENPLAY: **Stephen Gaghan,** *Traffic* • BEST FOREIGN LANGUAGE FILM: *Crouching Tiger, Hidden Dragon* • BEST SCORE: **Tan Dun,** *Crouching Tiger, Hidden Dragon* • BEST SONG: **Bob Dylan, "Things Have Changed,"** *Wonder Boys*

"Let's be honest: What's missing from tonight?" quipped Roberts (in Valentino) about her erstwhile *Erin Brockovich* cleavage.

Red-carpet onlookers saw all of Jennifer Lopez's sheer Chanel. But ABC kept cameras primly on her face during the telecast.

Unflapped by a kidnap threat and host Steve Martin's constant ribbing, Crowe gave a sincere speech in Armani and his grandpa's war medal.

A song nominee for *Dancer in the Dark*, Björk laid an egg (no, that was her purse) in a swan dress by Marjan Pejoski.

/ OSCARS / OSCARS / OSCARS / OSCARS / OSCARS / OSCARS / OSCARS / OSCARS / OSCARS / OSC.

"Nothing falling off or falling out," said three-time winner and practical gal Faith Hill (with husband Tim McGraw) of her coral Versace.

They hit the red carpet in Versace, but Destiny's Child accepted their awards in designs by Beyoncé Knowles' mother. Said Knowles (center, with Michelle Williams and Kelly Rowland): "She's the only person who knows what we want."

the grammys

A FEW OF THE 100 GOLDEN GRAMOPHONES AWARDED IN FEBRUARY...

RECORD OF THE YEAR: *Beautiful Day*, U2 ● ALBUM OF THE YEAR: *Two Against Nature*, Steely Dan ● SONG OF THE YEAR: *Beautiful Day*, U2 ● BEST POP VOCAL, FEMALE: *I Try*, Macy Gray ● BEST POP VOCAL, MALE: *She Walks This Earth*, Sting ● BEST POP VOCAL, GROUP: *Cousin Dupree*, Steely Dan ● BEST R&B ALBUM: *Voodoo*, D'Angelo ● BEST COUNTRY ALBUM: *Breathe*, Faith Hill ● BEST RAP ALBUM: *The Marshall Mathers LP*, Eminem ● BEST ROCK ALBUM: *There Is Nothing Left to Lose*, Foo Fighters ● BEST NEW ARTIST: Shelby Lynne

"It's a double-stick [tape] night," said winner Toni Braxton, explaining the physics of her well-ventilated extravaganza by Richard Tyler.

While some protested his nomination because of his album's slurs against gays, Eminem did a duet with the very out Elton John. "I think I've matured this year," said the rapper.

YS / GRAMMYS / GRAMMYS / GRAMMYS / GRAMMYS / GRAMMYS / GRAMMYS / GRAMM

the emmys

DRAMA SERIES: *The West Wing* ● COMEDY SERIES: *Sex and the City* ● ACTRESS, DRAMA: **Edie Falco**, *The Sopranos* ● ACTOR, DRAMA: **James Gandolfini**, *The Sopranos* ● ACTRESS, COMEDY: **Patricia Heaton**, *Everybody Loves Raymond* ● ACTOR, COMEDY: **Eric McCormack**, *Will & Grace* ● SUPPORTING ACTRESS, DRAMA: **Allison Janney**, *The West Wing* ● SUPPORTING ACTOR, DRAMA: **Bradley Whitford**, *The West Wing* ● SUPPORTING ACTRESS, COMEDY: **Doris Roberts**, *Everybody Loves Raymond* ● SUPPORTING ACTOR, COMEDY: **Peter MacNicol**, *Ally McBeal* ● VARIETY, MUSIC OR COMEDY SERIES: *Late Show with David Letterman* ● MINISERIES: *Anne Frank* ● MADE-FOR-TV MOVIE: *Wit* ● INDIVIDUAL PERFORMANCE IN A MUSIC OR VARIETY PROGRAM: **Barbra Streisand**, *Barbra Streisand: Timeless*

With many no-shows, presenters often had to accept on the winners' behalf. Martin Sheen was about to walk off with Judy Davis's Emmy when Steve Martin pulled a heist.

Ellen DeGeneres earned a standing ovation for hosting a night of pitch-perfect—and Björk-esque—gags.

Allison Janney was part of the *West Wing* landslide. Her short dress was in keeping with this year's "business casual" dress code.

"I didn't come to America for the weather, I came for this," said Canadian import Eric McCormack of his first trophy for *Will & Grace.*

Barbra Streisand didn't come out to receive her Emmy but provided an affecting surprise finale, singing "You'll Never Walk Alone."

'S / EMMYS / EMMYS / EMMYS / EMMYS / EMMYS / EMMYS / EMMYS / EMMYS / EMMYS

a pop-pourri...

HOLLYWOOD AND NASHVILLE CELEBRATE THE GOLDEN GLOBE AND CMA AWARDS

No man of constant sorrow, Toby Keith was crowned male vocalist of the year, his initial CMA win in five nominations.

Singer-songwriter Keith Urban became the first Australian to nab a CMA since Olivia Newton-John won way back in 1974.

"I wanted this so bad. And I have for so long," said Lee Ann Womack of her female vocalist of the year victory.

"This is actually a flask," joked George Clooney of his Globe. "I'll be proving that at the end of the night." No, Nicole Kidman wasn't his date. Clooney was with, he said, "my publicist, Stan."

Sarah Jessica Parker described her Ungaro gown as befitting "Ali MacGraw's 1971 Bel Air lifestyle."

GOLDEN GLOBES / GOLDEN GLOBES / GOLDEN GLOBES / GOLDEN GLOBES / GOLDEN G

The statuette season launched in January with the populist People's Choice Awards. There, *Friends'* Lisa Kudrow, David Schwimmer and Jennifer Aniston collected the show's second consecutive favorite TV comedy series honor.

Christina Aguilera shared the night's top prize, video of the year, with her "Lady Marmalade" collaborators: Pink, Mya, Lil' Kim and Missy Elliot.

...and more

HIGHLIGHTS FROM THE PEOPLE'S CHOICE AND MTV VIDEO MUSIC AWARDS

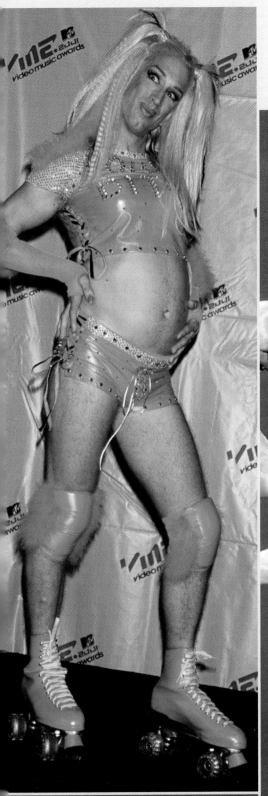

"I should call myself Pink. Oh, wait. That's taken," said comic Andy Dick, who introduced himself as Daphne Aguilera, Christina's little-known cousin.

Nominee Britney Spears went home empty-handed but had her paws full of unsubtle symbolism during a performance of "I'm a Slave 4 U."

TV / MTV / MTV / MTV / MTV / MTV / MTV / MTV / MTV / MTV / MTV / MTV / MTV / MTV / MTV / MT

CATHERINE ZETA-JONES / **MOST BEAUTIFUL**

"I may be the first actress to admit that beauty doesn't hold you back," says the Welsh stunner, 31. While Zeta-Jones isn't above enhancing her looks (she admits to being a "makeup fiend"), she wouldn't do any major changes: "I've got what I've got, and that's it."

people's
PEOPLE

Did your favorite stars turn up on the magazine's list of the Most Beautiful last year? Faith Hill did. Likewise Julia Roberts. What about your vote for Sexiest Man Alive? Ben Stiller earned a spot. Singer Maxwell too. Check out Jennifer Aniston and Leonardo DiCaprio as Best & Worst Dressed. Plus a lively mix of headliners and heroes became Most Intriguing People

ALEX RODRIGUEZ

The Texas Ranger shortstop, 25, says pal Gabrielle Reece, "actually becomes more attractive the longer you're around him."

HALLE BERRY

Though naturally blessed, Berry, 34, says beauty "takes work. If you take good care of yourself, you don't have to cover things up."

BEYONCÉ KNOWLES

Destiny's Child bandmates call Knowles, 19, the one the little girls want to look like. But it hasn't gone to her head. "I have many insecurities," she says. "They keep you humble."

MOST BEAUTIFUL PEOPLE

AMONG THE NIFTY 50 . . .

ACTRESS **Juliette Binoche** ● NBA PLAYER **Kobe Bryant** ● ACTRESS **Ellen Burstyn** ● FIRST LADY **Laura Bush** ● ACTOR **Chow Yun-Fat** ● ACTOR **George Clooney** ● TV HOST **Katie Couric** ● ACTRESS **Blythe Danner** ● ACTOR **Benicio Del Toro** ● ACTOR **Johnny Depp** ● ACTOR **Colin Firth** ● ACTOR **Ed Harris** ● ACTOR **Dulé Hill** ● SINGER **Faith Hill** ● ACTRESS **Kate Hudson** ● ACTOR **Hugh Jackman** ● MODEL **Heidi Klum** ● ACTOR **Jude Law** ● ACTOR **Heath Ledger** ● ACTRESS **Téa Leoni** ● SINGER/ACTRESS **Jennifer Lopez** ● ACTRESS **Debra Messing** ● ACTRESS **Julianne Moore** ● ACTRESS **Sydney Tamiia Poitier** ● TV HOST **Jeff Probst** ● TV HOST **Kelly Ripa** ● ACTRESS **Julia Roberts** ● ACTRESS **Julia Stiles** ● ACTOR **Noah Wyle** ● ACTRESS **Renée Zellweger** ● ACTRESS **Zhang Ziyi**

HEATHER LOCKLEAR

"She's a genetic freak," teases friend and makeup artist Lisa Ashley of the actress. "I think she gets better with age." It's 39.

TAYE DIGGS

"I can't believe I did that," says Diggs, 30, of the blond-streaked high-top fade haircut he sported as a teen. Even then, "my mother always told me I was handsome."

MOST INTRIGUING

The 25 who caught the editors' eye with their heroism, charisma or sheer audacity

A FEW OF THE CLASS OF 2001

COMMANDER-IN-CHIEF **George W. Bush** • *GLITTER*-ATI **Mariah Carey** • HEART OF LATE NIGHT **David Letterman** • CRISIS MANAGER **Rudolph Giuliani** • FOUNDING FATHER **John Adams** • ANCHOR **Katie Couric** • GOLDEN GIRL **Julia Roberts** • EYE OF A STORM **Gary Condit** • MUSICAL MADMAN **Mel Brooks** • PSYCHIC FRIEND **John Edward** • ROYAL UPSTART **Prince Harry** • SLUGGER **Barry Bonds** • WORKING MOM **Madonna**

DIANA KRALL

Krall, 37, became the top-selling jazz artist with a blend of sultry vocals and keyboard chops. "She swings," says fan Tony Bennett. "And, as I'm sure you've noticed, she's also very beautiful."

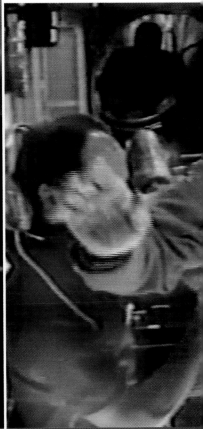

DENNIS TITO

What would you do with a spare $20 mil? This L.A. financier, 60, bought an eight-day spin on a Russian spacecraft.

REESE WITHERSPOON

A mom of Ava, 2, with Ryan Phillippe, 27, Witherspoon, 25, denies she's coddled like her *Legally Blonde* alter ego: "I don't think it's a joke that people put up $20 million for a movie. I show up. I know my lines."

KIM CATTRALL

"At this point in my life, I expected to be playing moms and wives," said Cattrall, 45. Instead, she is *Sex and the City*'s most intrepid single gal.

PIERCE BROSNAN

Under the flinty James Bond exterior, 2001's Sexiest Man Alive is a softy. According to his mum, Brosnan, 49, "crumbled a bit" at his August wedding to Keely Shaye Smith.

JOHN STAMOS

A former *General Hospital* regular, Stamos, 38, earns "sexiest comeback" honors for the prime-time hit *Thieves*.

SEXIEST MAN

PEOPLE travels the world to harvest another season's bounty of heartthrobs

IN 2001 THEY WERE THE HUNKIEST . . .

AUTHOR: **Robert Crais** • PITCHMAN: **Brian Baker** • NEWS CORRESPONDENT: **Nic Robertson** • CLASSICAL MUSICIAN: **Yo-Yo Ma** • SOAP STAR: **Jacob Young** • SOUL SINGER: **Maxwell** • WORLD LEADER: **Vicente Fox** • COUNTRY SINGER: **Brad Paisley** • CHEF: **Thomas Keller** • ATHLETES: **Tiki & Ronde Barber** • IMPORT: **Ioan Gruffudd** • RACE CAR DRIVER: **Helio Castroneves** • BUSINESSMAN: **Keith Clinkscales** • SHARK EXPERT: **Rocky Strong** • SELF-HELP GURU: **Phil McGraw**

BENJAMIN BRATT

"My intention is to make her the mother of my children," said "sexiest single guy" Bratt, 38, of the next woman he dates.

MATHEW ST. PATRICK

Before heading for the *Six Feet Under* set, St. Patrick, 33, the "sexiest newcomer," rises at 4 a.m. to read the Bible and hit the gym.

MARC ANTHONY

Perhaps surprisingly, "sexiest salsa singer" Anthony, 33, collects presidential letters, from Washington to Clinton.

BEST & WORST DRESSED

BEST
JENNIFER ANISTON

BEST
GEORGE CLOONEY

BEST
SARAH JESSICA PARKER

In firecracker-red Prada, Aniston set off sparks at the Emmy Awards. "I just went with what fit," she said.

"He looked like Cary Grant," said stylist Jeanne Yang of Clooney at a fund-raiser in turtleneck and suit. To her, the combo was "old-school glamor."

Defying the tide of flowing ball gowns at the Oscars, the *Sex and the City* star went for minimal coverage by Calvin Klein.

A sampler of celeb winners and sinners of the year 2001

WORST

LEONARDO DICAPRIO

Scruffy and wrinkled in L.A., DiCaprio could stand some lessons from his girlfriend, model Gisele Bündchen.

WORST

DIANE KEATON

Mistaking the premiere of *The Score* for a baby boomers' sock hop, Keaton made a misstep doing the time warp.

WORST

CHRISTINA AGUILERA

For the Blockbuster Awards, the singer appeared in a fright wig and a Mara Hoffman creation, with perhaps a little help from a paper shredder.

TRIBUTES

The world said a bittersweet farewell to Jack Lemmon, Perry Como, Katharine Graham, Dale Evans, Aaliyah and so many other luminaries who enriched our lives

Those were the days: when Carroll O'Connor's lovable blowhard ruled prime time from an easy chair

A racist and sexist, Archie Bunker "wasn't very likable," observed O'Connor. "But everybody loved him." *All in the Family*'s patriarch from Queens in no way resembled the liberal Manhattan-born actor who played him for 13 seasons. Premiering in 1971, *Family* was unprecedented in its language, subject matter (from Vietnam to homosexuality) and pioneering use of the audible toilet flush. Later, O'Connor launched (and won a fifth Emmy for) *In the Heat of the Night,* a series that featured a Southern cop involved with a black woman. (His first interracial TV kiss, however, came earlier, when Archie got smooched by Sammy Davis Jr.) O'Connor and Nancy, his wife of 50 years, raised a son, Hugh, also an actor. After battling addiction, Hugh committed suicide at 32 in 1995, and O'Connor became an antidrug advocate who sued his son's dealer. The tragedy shattered O'Connor, though he went on to play Helen Hunt's father on *Mad About You* in the late '90s. But until his death from a heart attack at 76, fans invariably greeted O'Connor with a rousing "Archie!"

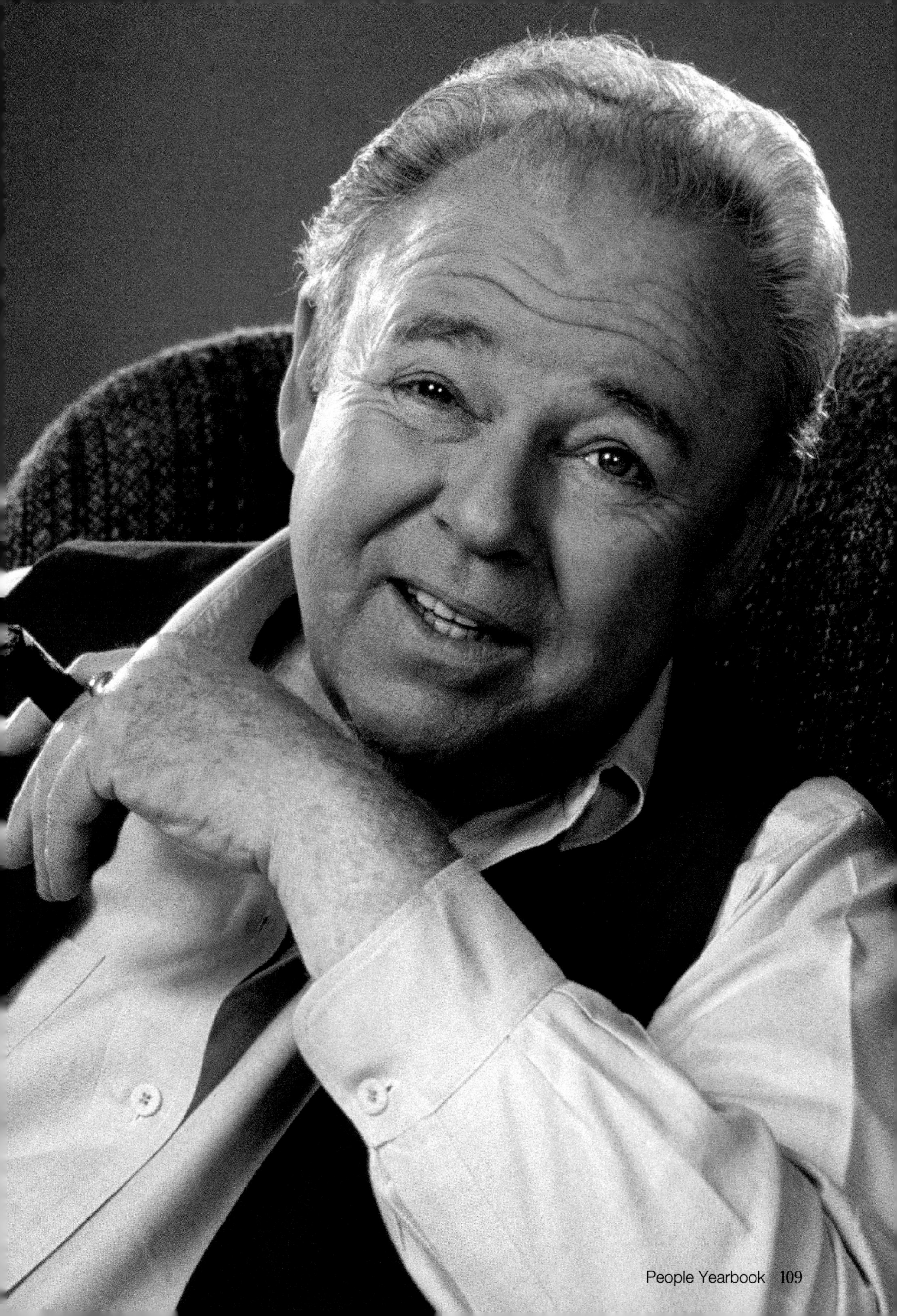

Jack
Lemmon

He was the ultimate working stiff: a hapless office drone in *The Apartment,* a desperate garment exec in *Save the Tiger,* a real estate salesman facing the ax in *Glengarry Glen Ross.* Rarely appearing in period pieces (*Some Like It Hot,* set in the '20s, was an exception), Lemmon was America's most contemporary actor in the second half of the last century. His choices mirrored the culture, from the bongo-playing beatnik in 1958's *Bell, Book and Candle* to the nuclear engineer in *The China Syndrome* (which opened just before the 1979 Three Mile Island accident) to the grumpy old man confronting the senior dating scene in *Out to Sea* (1997). In most roles the puckish two-time Oscar winner seemed either comically or tragically on the verge. He was a "choirboy with quiet hysteria seeping out of every pore," said Walter Matthau, Lemmon's *Odd Couple* costar and friend of 40 years. (The only person Lemmon spent more time with was his second wife, Felicia Farr, whom he wed in 1962.)

The two men were, in life, an unlikely pair. Matthau came from poor immigrants. Lemmon was a scion of New England wealth who graduated from Andover and Harvard. But he was an unspoiled star whom colleagues connived to work with. Billy Wilder directed him seven times. Neil Simon scripted four of his films. Kevin Spacey, whom he mentored, partnered with him in four, Matthau 11. A year after Matthau's passing, Lemmon, 76, succumbed to cancer. His last film was 2000's *The Legend of Bagger Vance,* and just before the first take, he quietly uttered the words with which he always began a shoot: "It's magic time."

Imogene Coca

Though Sid Caesar's *Your Show of Shows* boasted TV's best writers (Woody Allen, Mel Brooks), its pliable leading lady could reduce viewers to hysterics without a word. For 90 live minutes a week in the '50s, Coca's expressive antics helped addict the nation to a new medium. Born to an orchestra conductor and a vaudevillian, Coca became a master satirist. She skewered films (including a famous soggy spoof of *From Here to Eternity*), dance (Lily Tomlin admits to stealing her choreography) and opera (said diva Risë Stevens: "You're always deathly afraid the young singer will never make the last note. With Imogene, you're always afraid she will"). Twice widowed, Coca died in her Connecticut home at 92.

Joey Ramone

They never broke the Top 40. They weren't pretty enough to be on MTV (if they even had wanted to). But for two decades the punk granddaddies from Queens thrilled fans with manic performances of songs like "I Wanna Be Sedated" and "Blitzkrieg Bop." Led by Joey Ramone, a 6'3" stick insect behind a wall of hair, the Ramones took on 1970s arena rock and disco. (Their adopted surname came from a Paul McCartney alias.) Like the Beatles before them, the Ramones inspired generations of bands: the Sex Pistols, the Clash, U2, Nirvana. Born Jeffrey Hyman, Ramone, 49, died of lymphoma not far from the New York City club where his band, said *The Village Voice*, had tried to "blow a hole in the ozone layer."

John Lee Hooker

"He sounded like everything your parents didn't want you to have," said Bonnie Raitt. Hooker, one of 11 siblings, was raised in Mississippi, first by a preacher father who condemned his son's passion for the blues and then a stepdad who gave him a guitar. At 14, he took off for Memphis, and in 1948 he recorded "Boogie Chillen," showing off a stripped-down style with howling voice, a stomping foot and lyrics about love, lust and bad times. By the '70s Hooker had been overshadowed by acts like the Rolling Stones, Van Morrison and Carlos Santana—all of whom hailed his influence. In 1989 Santana and Raitt joined him on his album *The Healer*, which earned him his first of four Grammys, at age 72. He died at 83, a four-times-married father of eight children

Ray Walston

"I knew I was laying my career on the line," said Walston of signing on to play Uncle Martin, the curmudgeonly alien of *My Favorite Martian,* a mid-'60s sitcom. Indeed, the space-age role was Walston's best-known, a fact that irked him. The show, he griped, was "aimed at 5-year-olds." But grown-up film and theatergoers who knew Walston before his *Martian* days recalled his elegantly devilish Applegate in Broadway's *Damn Yankees,* for which he won a Tony, as well as parts in Tennessee Williams's *Summer and Smoke* and, onscreen, in *The Apartment.* With his wife of 57 years, their daughter and grandchildren at his side, Walston died at 86 from lupus. In his later years he had helped refine his TV legacy by winning two Emmys in four seasons of *Picket Fences,* on which he played a judge with a familiar cantankerous streak.

Dale Evans

"How that spurious cowhand can be content to kiss a horse when he has Miss Evans on the lot every day, I cannot imagine," wrote a critic of Roy Rogers. The two paired in more than 25 movies, starting with 1944's *The Cowboy and the Senorita,* and three years later Rogers became her fourth husband. Together they had a merged brood of 10 kids—plus their extended TV menagerie. Through the '50s, the smiling couple wished audiences "Happy Trails," in a song Evans had composed. Privately, they faced tragedy. Two of their children died in accidents, another from heart problems. By the time of her death (two years after Rogers's) at 88, the trials had moved Evans, a devout Christian, to a second career penning inspirational books.

Troy Donahue

"If Troy Donahue could be a movie star, then I could be a movie star. . . ." So went a biting lyric from *A Chorus Line*. But the teen idol who won roles with his blond rip-curl hair and Pacific-blue eyes might well have agreed. After winning fame in *A Summer Place* and TV's *Surfside 6*, Donahue, says friend Bob Palmer, "took his career lightly." When it evaporated in the late '60s, Donahue, born Merle Johnson in New York City, turned to drugs, sobering up only after spending a few months homeless in Central Park. Married four times, Donahue was engaged to a Chinese-born opera singer he'd met while teaching acting on a cruise ship. He died at 65, following a heart attack.

Willie Stargell

As a minor-leaguer from 1959 to 1962, Wilver Stargell (as he was born in Oklahoma) sometimes had to live apart from the white players. So for his 21 seasons with Pittsburgh, an era of ever-increasing diversity, the slugger made clubhouse unity his mission. Memorably, in 1979 he proclaimed Sister Sledge's "We Are Family" the team fight song, led the Pirates to a World Series win and became its MVP. The father of five, known as Pops by the baseball world, was voted into the game's Hall of Fame in his first year of eligibility. He died at 61 of a stroke.

Morton Downey Jr.

Sean Morton Downey Jr., the son of an Irish radio singer and an actress-dancer, dabbled in several careers before finding his voice. And when he did, it was a loud, shrill, in-your-face bellow. Downey, a Boston native, had been a singer for Dick Clark's Caravan of Stars, a disc jockey, a cofounder of the American Basketball Association, a lobbyist, a long-shot presidential candidate in 1980 and an aid worker who, after raising money to build hospitals in Nigeria, was knighted by Pope Paul VI. In the mid-'80s Downey turned to talk radio. His caustic style drew fans who tuned in to hear Downey rail against everyone from liberals to the Ku Klux Klan. In 1987 he adapted his show for cable and later went national with guests like skinheads and porn stars. In his short spell on the air, "Mort the Mouth" paved the way for schlock-talkers like Jerry Springer. But the father of four daughters from four marriages was, said Sally Jessy Raphaël, "as gentle as could be. The opposite of the man on TV." Once a four-pack-a-day smoker, Downey lost a lung to cancer in 1996 and became an antitobacco crusader. Then, at age 67, Downey's infamous mouth fell silent.

William Masters

Rarely have scientists been asked to share their findings on *The Tonight Show*, especially before Masters and Virginia Johnson in 1966. Dr. Masters purported to be "amazed" that their dry text landed them a spot on the bestseller list and a Carson invite. Anyone would be, if the subject hadn't been sex. Picking up the work of Alfred Kinsey, Masters and assistant Johnson (who became his second wife) published *Human Sexual Response*, an 11-year study of 694 men and women to demystify sex and make it more pleasurable. Where Kinsey relied on subjects' recollections, Masters observed lovers in the act. He and Johnson divorced in 1993, a year after their professional union ended. The father of two with his first wife, Masters wed again in 1993. Just before dying, from complications of Parkinson's disease at 85, he proved that his life's work hadn't ruined his romantic side by whispering to his wife, "You're a knockout."

Eudora Welty

A hungry reader, Welty was shocked as a girl to learn that "books had been written by people, that books were not natural wonders, coming up of themselves like grass." She grew up to create her own exquisitely rendered and often humorous tales of Southern gentility that earned her six O. Henry Awards and the 1973 Pulitzer for *The Optimist's Daughter*. Never married and residing most of her 92 years in the Jackson, Mississippi, house her father built, Welty was a master of the short story, closer stylistically to Chekhov than Faulkner, her Southern contemporary. One story, "Why I Live at the [Post Office]," would, five decades later, inspire a computer programmer to christen his popular e-mail program "Eudora."

Whitman Mayo

Two decades after *Sanford and Son* went into reruns, fans would approach Mayo, who played Sanford's sidekick Grady Wilson, to say he hadn't aged at all. He still seemed to be the same sixtysomething known for saying "Good goobily goop." In fact, Mayo was in his 40s when he took on the gray-bearded role, which he modeled on his own grandfather. Growing up in New York City, Mayo said he "got pleasure out of studying old people. Older folk are like children. They can do and say what they want and get away with it." After five years with *Sanford*, Mayo headlined a short-lived spinoff, *Grady*. Fearing that acting was an unreliable way to make a living, he opened a travel agency in Los Angeles. Later he would teach drama at Clark Atlanta University. But Mayo always worked steadily both on TV and in films like *Boyz N the Hood* and *Boycott*, an HBO movie about the Montgomery bus protest. Survived by his wife and three kids, Mayo, 70, said in 1999 of his trademark television role, "I finally grew into the part."

Douglas Adams

The notion occurred to him as he lay—on a break from school, and somewhat inebriated—in a field in Austria, looking at the stars and toting *The Hitchhiker's Guide to Europe*. Why wasn't there a similarly pragmatic tour book about space? So the onetime Monty Python collaborator pitched the idea to BBC radio. The resulting *Hitchhiker's Guide to the Galaxy* spun the comic adventures of Arthur Dent, an earthling; Ford Prefect, an alien disguised as an out-of-work actor; and Marvin, a depressive robot. The show led to a 1979 book that spawned four sequels (he called it a "five-part trilogy") and sold more than 14 million copies. Adams had created a fictional world right down to its physics. In one book he described spaceships as floating in the air "in exactly the same way that bricks don't." To make a film version of *Hitchhiker*, Adams moved from his native England to California. He died there not long after, at 49, of a heart attack while at a health club—but not before revealing for readers the answer to "life, the universe and everything": 42.

Jason Miller

His Pulitzer Prize-winning play *That Championship Season* depicted a reunion of high school basketball players who fear their best year is behind them. Miller might well have felt that way about 1973. Not only did he take drama's top honor but also earned an Oscar nod for portraying Father Damien Karras in *The Exorcist.* Miller subsequently wrote other plays, appeared in several films and directed a film version of *Season.* He died at 62 after a heart attack in his native Scranton, Pennsylvania, where he had been the artistic director of the local public theater since 1986. His four children (three with wife Linda, the daughter of Jackie Gleason; another with a girlfriend) include actor Jason Patric and author Joshua Miller, with whom he was writing a new play, titled *Me and My Old Man.*

Pauline Kael

"I'd rather be panned by Kael than praised by Rex Reed," said director Billy Wilder. Kael, the tough and influential movie critic for *The New Yorker* from 1968 to 1991, obliged Wilder several times. She didn't mince words (a scathing review of *The Sound of Music* reportedly got her fired from an earlier gig at *McCall's*) but earned the respect of readers and the cinema elite alike. Kael's longest love affair (she was married and divorced three times) was with the movies—a term she preferred to "film." She praised favorite stars like Marlon Brando, Diane Keaton and Denzel Washington while taking the air out of overblown blockbusters. One target, George Lucas, retaliated by naming a villain in *Willow* "General Kael." Survived by a daughter, Kael, 82, died at home in Massachusetts. A Berkeley philosophy grad, she published numerous volumes of collected reviews (among the titles: *I Lost It at the Movies*). Asked if she would ever write her memoirs, she replied, "I think I have."

Gunther Gebel-Williams

When he was 12, his mother, a German war widow, abandoned him at the circus. Young Gebel added the last name of the owner and apprenticed as an animal trainer. In the subsequent 43 years (the latter half with Ringling Bros.) he redefined the genre, tossing out whips and chairs and gently coaxing wild cats to ride on horseback, or elephants to be springboards for his somersaults. Although his bravery bought him numerous clawings and bites, he never missed a performance. Married twice and the father of two, Gebel-Williams died from cancer at 66, a decade after his son followed him into the ring.

Samuel Z. Arkoff

"We often would get the title first. Then we would work up a poster. If it looked good, we'd go ahead with a script." That was the Arkoff formula. And the titles with which he started—*How to Stuff a Wild Bikini, Ghost of Dragstrip Hollow, I Was a Teenage Werewolf*—led to features that could be shot in a week on a minuscule budget, virtually guaranteeing his profits. In his 200-plus productions, the Iowa native turned B-movie mogul launched the careers of Roger Corman (*The Undead*), Francis Ford Coppola (*Dementia 13*) and Martin Scorsese (*Boxcar Bertha*). Cashing in on trends from beach romps in the '60s to blaxploitation films in the '70s to horror flicks in the '80s never won Arkoff, who died at 83, any major awards. But it did get him a Museum of Modern Art retrospective. His reaction? "I suppose time can dignify anything."

Christopher Hewett

In the tradition of Wooster's Jeeves, or Arthur's Hobson, Mr. Belvedere was a starchy British butler—superior in every way to those he served. For six TV seasons, Mr. Belvedere (did he *have* a first name?) was played to withering perfection by Hewett. The conceit of his 1980s sitcom had the veddy proper Belvedere waiting on a dysfunctional American clan. Like his alter ego, Hewett, a native of Worthing, England, cast a harsh eye on his three young costars (that's Brice Beckham, right) if they chewed gum on the set. He himself first took the stage at 7 in *A Midsummer Night's Dream*. ("No lines, but lots of lovely costumes," he recalled.) Hewett, who never married and died at 80 from complications of diabetes, created one other indelible character: the over-the-top director Roger De Bris in Mel Brooks's 1968 film *The Producers*.

Anne Morrow Lindbergh

Though half of prewar America's most admired couple, Anne Lindbergh was a remarkably accomplished individual. The New Jersey native wrote more than two dozen books of poetry, prose and journals chronicling her travels with Charles Lindbergh, whom she wed in 1929, two years after his historic Atlantic flight. The first woman to earn a glider pilot's license, she was his navigator on route-charting trips to Europe, Asia and the Caribbean. Her most widely read work, *Gift from the Sea,* addressed modern women, whom she called "the great vacationless class," from the perspective of a mother of six. In 1932 the Lindberghs' first child was kidnapped and murdered, which crushed Lindbergh and strained her marriage. She would later have a brief affair with French aviator Antoine de Saint-Exupéry. Outliving her husband by a quarter century, Lindbergh died at 94, after suffering multiple strokes which left her able to recall only shards of her extraordinary life.

Perry Como

He "invented casual," said Bing Crosby of Como, a singer beloved as much for his easygoing manner as for his easy-listening baritone. Raised by Italian parents in blue-collar Pennsylvania, Pierino Como was content as a young man to be a barber, marry his high school girlfriend, Roselle Belline, and sing weekends for the local Sons of Italy chapter. But a touring big band auditioned him and enlisted his smooth, if untutored, voice. By all reports, the cardigan-wearing Como changed very little, even as he scored hits through the '40s and '50s with ballads ("Some Enchanted Evening") as well as novelties ("Hot Diggity"). When rock displaced his crooning contemporaries, Como carried on, hosting a long-running TV variety show and Christmas specials into the 1980s. When he died at 88, pal Tony Bennett remembered Como as "the only sane singer in the world, including myself."

Dorothy McGuire

As a teen in Indianapolis, McGuire played the Virgin Mary in a school play. It was prescient casting, for McGuire would build a career lending her wholesome visage as the mother characters in *Swiss Family Robinson, Old Yeller, A Tree Grows in Brooklyn* and, in a reprise of that early role, as Mary in *The Greatest Story Ever Told*. In between, she tested her versatility as Gregory Peck's liberal fiancée in *Gentleman's Agreement* and as a vamp in *Till the End of Time,* after which, she said, "I went right back to playing nice girls and faithful wives." She married photographer John Swope and was a mom of two. He died in 1979, and McGuire rarely worked the last of her 85 years. But by then, longtime colleague Norman Lloyd had characterized her film legacy as "the best in what we would conjure up as a perfect American woman."

Robert Ludlum

"A lousy book," said one reviewer of a Ludlum tome. "I stayed up until 3 a.m. to finish it." Another unimpressed critic admitted to having "sprained my wrist turning his pages." Though Ludlum didn't begin his writing career until giving up stage acting and producing at the advanced age of 42, the native New Yorker quickly found his market niche. Critics gagged, but the public lapped him up, buying more than 200 million copies of his 21 titles, beginning with 1971's *The Scarlatti Inheritance,* which imagined the financiers who backed the Nazi party. Preferring the term "novels of paranoia" to "thrillers," Ludlum hooked readers with tales of spies, counterspies and the femmes fatales with whom they kept company between plot twists. Married to a college girlfriend, Mary Ryducha, Ludlum, a father of three, was widowed in 1996 and rewed before dying at 73 of a heart attack. Although his writing allowed him to give up an unfulfilling acting career, he would play one final role—a wealthy author in an American Express ad.

John Phillips

Raised on the 1950s harmonies of the Modernaires by a Marine father and a Cherokee Indian mother, Phillips would orchestrate four voices that defined mid-'60s West Coast flower power. With second wife Michelle, Denny Doherty and Cass Elliot, Phillips's group, the Mamas and the Papas, lured a hippie nation west, from the Greenwich Village folk scene to the loving warmth they romanticized in "California Dreamin'." After five albums the band broke up, as did his marriage. Through the '70s, Papa John dulled his genius with heroin and alcohol, which later necessitated a liver transplant. When he died, at 65, he was mourned by a generation, as well as four wives, two sons and three daughters: the performers MacKenzie, Chynna and Bijou. The night of his memorial, the marquee at the Roxy on Sunset Boulevard captured the feeling in L.A. by reading, simply, "All the leaves are brown and the sky is grey."

Ann Sothern

At RKO and Columbia, she was the Queen of the B's, turning out 18 pictures in three years. At MGM she was Maisie, a determined chorus girl, in a series so successful that when she tried to walk away, Louis B. Mayer told her, sorry, "your movies pay for our mistakes." Like her pal Lucille Ball, she left a busy but unsatisfying film career for TV. A canny businesswoman, Sothern produced and made millions from her own series, *Private Secretary* and *The Ann Sothern Show*. The twice-married actress, who died at 92, returned to the screen for an Oscar-nominated role in 1987's *The Whales of August*. Its director, Lindsay Anderson, recalled her as "too good an actress to be a star."

John Hartford

Nimble with a banjo or fiddle, Hartford was a musician and historian of folk and bluegrass who underestimated his own eminence in the field. Raised in St. Louis, he was a session player in Nashville when Chet Atkins discovered him for RCA. In 1967 Hartford had an originally modest hit with "Gentle on My Mind." But covered by everyone from Glen Campbell (who, like its composer, won two Grammys with it) to Aretha Franklin to Frank Sinatra, the song became radio's second most-played tune, after the Beatles' "Yesterday." Yet as success grew, Hartford yearned for a simpler life. He had proved his comic chops on the Smothers Brothers' TV show but turned down a CBS detective series. He resettled with his wife in Nashville, raising a son, playing music and piloting a riverboat, the *Julia Belle Swain*. Before losing a long battle with cancer at 63, Hartford brought his traditional twang to the soundtrack of *O Brother, Where Art Thou?*

Maureen Reagan

"ERA" read the campaign buttons Maureen Reagan designed in 1980. Closer up, they said, "Elect Reagan Anyway." It was a daughter's lovingly subversive way of disagreeing with her candidate father over the Equal Rights Amendment. The pin was classic Maureen—never afraid to speak her mind, even when in conflict with her family. (Unlike her dad, she was a pro-choice feminist and believed that Oliver North should have been court-martialed.) The older of two children from Ronald Reagan's marriage to Jane Wyman, Maureen followed her father into acting and later into politics, with two unsuccessful congressional bids. Still, she wielded power, chairing the Republican Women's Political Action League. Details of the Wyman-Reagan divorce helped sell her memoir. But for her the book was a tool to speak out against domestic abuse, of which she had been a victim in her first marriage. Alzheimer's research was her agenda when she died at 60 from skin cancer, survived by third husband Dennis Revell and daughter Rita.

Anthony Quinn

He was a Chihuahua-born blend of Mexican and Irish parentage, but over a seven-decade film career played Indian, Eskimo, Hawaiian, Chinese and, notably, Greek. With 1964's *Zorba,* Quinn found a persona-defining role. The character's bouzouki dance—eyes closed in rapture, arms outstretched to the sun—offered an apt metaphor for the actor's embrace of life, which he described in two candid volumes of autobiography. He lived big, trying his hand at boxing, saxophone and preaching before settling on acting (and occasional painting). He fathered 13 children, had three wives and publicized affairs with Rita Hayworth, Ingrid Bergman and Bergman's daughter Pia Lindstrom. The son of Mexican revolutionaries who fled to raise their son in East L.A., he won his first Oscar for *Viva Zapata!,* playing the brother of the opposition leader. Before his death of respiratory failure at 86, he capped a film résumé which included *Lawrence of Arabia* and Fellini's *La Strada* with a Broadway-musical version of *Zorba,*

Chet Atkins

"Trying to get it right" was the plain-spoken answer the guitar virtuoso gave when folks asked why he continued performing after 60 years. Raised poor in Tennessee—he'd restring his banjo with wire from a screen door—Atkins invented a thumb-and-three-finger picking style with which he could play two melodies at once. He went on to win 14 Grammys and had a great ear for business. As a producer and executive for RCA Victor, Atkins adapted country music to changing public tastes, creating what became known as the Nashville Sound. He was instrumental in developing the careers of legends like Waylon Jennings, Roger Miller and Dolly Parton, and it was Atkins who persuaded RCA to outbid Columbia and sign Elvis Presley. Married for 55 years, Atkins died at 77 from cancer at home in Nashville, the city he had put on music's map.

Christiaan Barnard

Though medically plausible, taking a heart from a human donor was long considered ethically questionable. Thus South African surgeon Barnard made history in 1967, when a young woman, hit by a car, lost brain function while her heart continued to beat. Barnard harvested the organ and placed it in the chest of terminal heart patient Louis Washkansky, 55, who lived for 18 days before dying from pneumonia. (Barnard, a foe of apartheid, later dramatically transplanted a black man's heart into a white man, who survived 19 months.) The transplant procedure is now common, and 75 percent of recipients live at least five years. Barnard, who died from asthma at 78, wound up a world celeb, marrying and divorcing three times and squiring high-profile girlfriends, including Gina Lollobrigida.

Katharine Graham

Her father believed that a man shouldn't have his wife as a boss. So he passed the stewardship of *The Washington Post* to son-in-law Philip Graham. A young reporter, Kay Graham accepted the arrangement—and her life as a socialite and mother of four. But when Philip, a depressive, committed suicide in 1963, she reluctantly succeeded him to keep the *Post* in the family, remaking herself from a self-described "doormat" to the nation's most powerful woman. In doing so, she elevated a third-rate daily to journalistic prominence, fearlessly publishing the Pentagon Papers, which revealed the government's manipulations in Vietnam, and the Watergate investigation that led to Richard Nixon's resignation. Before her death at 84 after injuries from a fall, she won a Pulitzer herself for *Personal History,* a powerful memoir and testament to her changing times. Throughout, she maintained her status as D.C.'s best-loved salon hostess. Never wed again, Graham noted, "When you live alone, you're married to your friends."

Arlene Francis

She was best known as a perennial panelist on prime time's longest-running game show, *What's My Line?*, in which celebrity inquisitors tried to guess a guest's profession. But what if Francis (here, in 1952, with *Line* host John Daly) had been a contestant? "Ever been onstage?" Yes, with Orson Welles. "Made any films?" Several, beginning with 1932's *Murders in the Rue Morgue* with Bela Lugosi. "How about radio?" Yes, she had her own show from 1960 to 1984. Born Arline Kazanjian in Boston, Francis enjoyed a more varied career than was suggested by her 25 years posing coy questions to *Line* visitors. Her trademark was a heart-shaped diamond pendant, a gift from her husband, actor Martin Gabel. Francis, who died at 93, retired before symptoms of Alzheimer's disease began to slow her famously sharp wit.

FRANCIS

Glenn Hughes

In 1977 New York City toll collector Hughes answered an ad calling for "gay singers and dancers, very good-looking and with mustaches." He got the gig and, with five bandmates, adopted onstage personae based on male stereotypes: a soldier, a construction worker, a cowboy, an Indian, a police officer. Hughes, in oiled black leather and chains, was the biker. Though the Village People had aspired only to conquer the gay club scene, they got huge radio play in 1978 with "Macho Man." Other hits like "Y.M.C.A." moved 65 million records and inspired a 1980 film, *Can't Stop the Music.* Hughes left the band in 1996, and lung cancer took him at 50. But the Village People still tour with a rotating lineup, and camp classics like "In the Navy" remain popular in the era of "Don't ask, don't tell."

Isaac Stern

The violin, said Stern, "talks from the heart. It can laugh, it can cry. It is really a way of speaking." From his debut at 16, Stern used the instrument to speak volumes. Born in the Ukraine and raised in San Francisco, he eventually settled in Manhattan and in 1951 became the first American violinist to tour the Soviet Union. Later he boycotted that nation until it allowed artists the freedom to travel. A supporter of Israel, Stern joined Leonard Bernstein and the Israel Philharmonic soon after the Six-Day War in 1967. During the Gulf War, in 1991, he rehearsed with the orchestra in a gas mask. At home he used his clout to help save Carnegie Hall from destruction in 1960 and co-founded the National Endowment for the Arts. A twice-divorced father of three, Stern, 81, mentored Yo-Yo Ma, Emanuel Ax and many others. "Our job as musicians," he told them, "is to always remind people of how beautiful things can be."

Korey Stringer

"The hardest thing I had to do was ask him to be a tough guy," said Minnesota Vikings offensive line coach Mike Tice of Stringer. "He was a teddy bear." The 335-lb. teddy bear wound up a Pro Bowl tackle. Off the field, Stringer, 27, also pulled his weight. An All-American at Ohio State, he was beloved in his adopted Minnesota home, where he founded Korey's Crew, a community program. Beyond funding the campaign, the father (with wife Kelci) of Kodie, 3, often visited grade-schoolers to encourage reading. Then, on a scorching preseason practice day in July, Stringer's exertion caused his body temperature to rise to 108°, leading to his death and to an NFL review of training-camp rules. At a memorial in his birthplace, Warren, Ohio, one observer noted that although mourners were filled with warm recollections about Stringer, not a single one mentioned football.

Lani O'Grady

Growing up in a showbiz family, Lani O'Grady should have been comfortable enough in front of the cameras. Her mother, Mary Grady (Lani added the *O* to her stage name), was a top children's talent agent, and her brother Don grew up as an original Mouseketeer and starred in *My Three Sons*. Visiting Don on the set of the latter show, Lani thought she might like to try acting. She broke out as a teenager, playing eldest daughter Mary Bradford on the '70s series *Eight Is Enough*. But despite being around TV soundstages much of her young life, O'Grady was constantly anxious at work, and began relying on Valium or other tranquilizers to calm herself down. When the show ended in 1981, O'Grady's résumé thinned to a few TV films, *Love Boat* appearances and *Eight Is Enough* reunion movies. The major work of her adulthood seemed to be battling her addiction to painkillers and alcohol. She was 46, recently sober and thinking about returning to acting, said her mother, when she died at her Valencia, California, home, of natural causes.

Hank Ketcham

"Your son is a menace," Alice Ketcham blared at her husband. Their 4-year-old, Dennis, had just torn apart his bedroom. Inspired, the illustrator, previously employed by Disney, took up his pen, and in 1951 created a character named for his mischievous son. Within three years *Dennis the Menace* had 30 million readers. The real Dennis grew up more troubled than Dennis Mitchell, who later appeared on TV and in film. His mother died of a drug overdose when he was 12, and after a difficult tour in Vietnam he became estranged from his father. The elder Ketcham, who died at 81 of cancer, called their relationship "just a chapter . . . that closed." The book has yet to close on the cartoon Dennis, who, with the help of other artists, continues to pester Mr. Wilson.

Aaliyah

From the time she was 11 and onstage in Las Vegas with her aunt Gladys Knight, Aaliyah Dana Haughton didn't want folks to think of her as too young. She coyly titled her debut album *Age Ain't Nothing but a Number,* as if to suggest that at 15 she was ready for the grown-up success her sultry voice would bring. By 2001 the Brooklyn-born, Detroit-raised performer was a veteran in the music business, with two Grammy nominations and two platinum albums. She had also moved into film, costarring in *Romeo Must Die,* playing the title role in *The Queen of the Damned* and signing on for two *Matrix* sequels. But she never let incipient superstardom take her far from her parents, Diane and Michael Haughton, or her brother Rashad. Those who worked with her admired her solidity. "She exuded confidence without being arrogant or unpleasant," said producer Curtis Waller. It was easy to forget she was only 22. But when a small plane taking her home from a video shoot crashed in the Bahamas, killing Aaliyah and eight others, all her fans could say was that she was just too young.

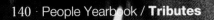

George Harrison

At 14, he pestered schoolmate Paul McCartney to let him in his band. On an $8 guitar, he taught John Lennon (far left) to play. As the Beatles hit big, Harrison was dwarfed by its main composers but did write classics like "Here Comes the Sun" and, for first wife Pattie Boyd, the gorgeous "Something." Divorced after 11 years, he wed Olivia Arias in 1978 and had a son, Dhani. A sitar solo on "Norwegian Wood" hinted at his lifelong love of India. After the Beatles bid *namaste* to the maharishi, Harrison remained devoted to Hinduism. Though dubbed "the mystical one," he was a grounded businessman and creator of the first charity mega-concerts in 1971, to benefit famine-stricken Bangladesh. Friends also thought "the quiet one" a misnomer. "He never stopped talking when I was with him," said Monty Python's Michael Palin. (Harrison produced his *Life of Brian* and other films.) Preferring to tend the grounds of his Friar Park estate, the first ex-Beatle with a No. 1 single, "My Sweet Lord," insisted that "I don't want to be in the business full-time. I'm a gardener." While he disparagingly called his band the Fabs, Harrison, 58, who died of cancer, also said, "We had the time of our lives. We laughed for years."

picture credits

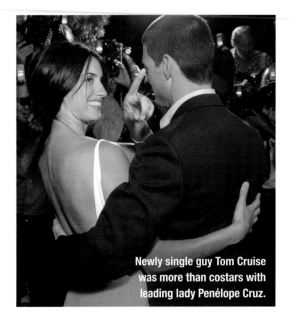

Newly single guy Tom Cruise was more than costars with leading lady Penélope Cruz.

MAZUR/WIREIMAGE; (top) STEPHEN SCRENCI **40-41** (clockwise from top right) SHAWN BALDWIN/AP; ALDEN PELLETT/THE IMAGE WORKS; STEPHEN J. CARRERA/AP; GETTY IMAGES **42-43** LOU DEMATTEIS/SIPA PRESS **44-45** (clockwise from right) REUTERS/POOL; HARLAND BRAUN/AP; JUSTIN SULLIVAN/AP; FBI/AP **46-47** (clockwise from top right) ERICA BERGER; TODD FRANCE; VIRGINIA SHERWOOD/ABC **48-49** (from left) NICK UT/AP; DIDIER FEREY/GETTY IMAGES; PAUL SANCYA/AP **50-51** MICHAEL GRIECO

hot properties

52-53 THEO WESTENBERGER **54-55** CHRIS HASTON/NBC **56-57** (clockwise from left) DANNY TURNER; RON DAVIS/SHOOTING STAR; SCOTT WACHTER/TIMEPIX **58-59** (from left) DEBORAH FEINGOLD; DAVE MARTIN/AP **60-61** (clockwise from left) STEVE LABADESSA; RAFAEL FUCHS; NICKELODEON **62-63** (from left) ERICA BERGER; ANTHONY MANDLER/CORBIS OUTLINE **64-65** PETER MOUNTAIN/WARNER BROS.

milestones

66-67 JOE BUISSINK/REUTERS/GETTY IMAGES **68-69** (from left) GREG GORMAN AND RICHARD MARCHISOTTO © KILKENNY PRODUCTIONS; MARTIN GRIMES/SPLASH; LOUIE D **70-71** (from left) JOE BUISSINK/WIREIMAGE; GREG MATHIESON/MAI PHOTO NEWS AGENCY; DAVID SCHUMACHER **72-73** (from left) HENRY MCGEE/GLOBE PHOTOS; KEVIN WINTER/IMAGE DIRECT; LISA MAIZLISH/ZUMA PRESS **74-75** (from left) JOE BUISSINK/AP; DERRINGER & WEITZ/GETTY IMAGES **76-77** (from left) NEAL PRESTON/CORBIS OUTLINE; BERLINER/BEI **78-79** (clockwise from top right) AGASSI ENTERPRISES INC./AP; FAME PICTURES; BIG PICTURES USA; VALERIE BLUM/REFLEX NEWS **80-81** (from left) DIANE FREED/GETTY IMAGES; DAVID KEELER/ONLINE USA **82-83** (from left) SPLASH; UK PRESS; GETTY IMAGES; CHRIS MOODY/HUTCHINS PHOTO **84-85** (from left) TAMMIE ARROYO/IPOL; TERRY LILLY/ZUMA PRESS; MARION CURTIS/DMI

hollywood's big nights

86-87 MIKE BLAKE/GETTY IMAGES **88-89** (from left) DONATO SARDELLA/WWD; RAMEY PHOTO AGENCY; MIREK TOWSKI/DMI/TIMEPIX; FRED PROUSER/REUTERS/GETTY IMAGES **90-91** (from left) LISA ROSE/JPI; DAVE ALLOCA/DMI/TIMEPIX; LISA ROSE/JPI; GARY HERSHORN/REUTERS/GETTY IMAGES **92-93** (from left) GETTY IMAGES; KEVIN WINTER/IMAGE DIRECT; LISA ROSE/JPI; TAMMIE ARROYO/GETTY IMAGES **94-95** (from left) TAMMIE ARROYO; LISA ROSE/JPI; TAMMIE ARROYO; CHRIS DELMASZ/UMA PRESS; TAMMIE ARROYO/RETNA LTD. **96-97** (from left) SIPA PRESS; ARIEL RAMIREZ/HUTCHINS PHOTO; RETNA LTD.; KEVIN KANE/WIREIMAGE

people's people

98-99 JIM WRIGHT/ICON **100-101** (clockwise from right) BOB FRAME/LAMOINE AGENCY; MARK LIDDELL/ICON; ART STREIBER/ICON; NICK BARATTA/TEEN PEOPLE; ISABEL SNYDER/CORBIS OUTLINE **102-103** (clockwise from right) STEVE SANDS; ITAR-TASS/CORBIS SYGMA; BOB FRAME; CHRIS PIZZELLO/AP **104-105** (from left) COLIN BELL; MOSHE BRAKHA/ABC; ANTHONY MANDLER; SANDRA JOHNSON; NICK BARATTA **106-107** (from left) PAUL SMITH/RETNA LTD.; CHRIS WEEKS/GETTY IMAGES; AXELLE/BAUER/GRIFFIN; JOHNATHAN MOFFAT/ZUMA PRESS; KEVIN WINTER/IMAGE DIRECT; STEVE GRANITZ/WIREIMAGE

tributes

108-109 GABI RONA/CBS PHOTO ARCHIVE **110-111** LARRY BARBIER JR./GLOBE PHOTOS **112-113** (from left) LARRY BARBIER JR./GLOBE PHOTOS; STEPHEN DANELIAN/CORBIS OUTLINE **114-115** (from left) RETNA LTD.; PHOTOFEST **116-117** (from left) PHOTOFEST; KOBAL COLLECTION **118-119** (clockwise from left) PHOTOFEST; GEORGE LANGE/CORBIS OUTLINE; PAUL OCKRASSA/AP **120-121** (clockwise from left) NANCY R. SCHIFF/GETTY IMAGES; IPOL; ED KASHI/GETTY IMAGES **122-123** (clockwise from right) FELD ENTERTAINMENT; DEBORAH FEINGOLD/HULTON ARCHIVE/GETTY IMAGES; BRIAN HAMILL/GETTY IMAGES **124-125** (clockwise from right) INP; ABC PHOTO ARCHIVES; STEVE LABADESSA **126-127** (clockwise from left) GLOBE PHOTOS; BOB LANDRY/TIMEPIX; PETER FRONTH **128-129** (from left) MICHAEL OCHS ARCHIVE; GABI RONA/MPTV **130-131** (clockwise from right) GLOBE PHOTOS; NICK UT/AP; MARK HUMPHREY/AP **132-133** (clockwise from right) COURTESY GRAHAM FAMILY; GAMMA; RETNA LTD. **134-135** (clockwise from top right) TOM ANSLEY/GLOBE PHOTOS; FRANK MICELOTTA/CORBIS OUTLINE; CBS PHOTO ARCHIVE **136-137** (clockwise from right) AP PHOTO; CARLOS GONZALEZ/MINNEAPOLIS STAR TRIBUNE/REUTERS; WARNER BROS. **138-139** KHAREN HILL/WARNER BROS. **140-141** CURT GUNTHER/LONDON FEATURES

cover

FRONT COVER CHARLES KRUPA/AP; (insets, from top) JEFF MITCHELL/REUTERS/GETTY IMAGES; AVIK GILBOA/WIREIMAGE; MARK J. TERRILL/AP; PETER MOUNTAIN/WARNER BROS.; FITZROY BARRETT/GLOBE PHOTOS; PETER BROOKER/REX FEATURES **BACK COVER** (row 1, from left) PAUL SMITH/FEATUREFLASH; GEOFF WILKINSON; FASHION WIRE DAILY; KEVIN MAZUR/WIREIMAGE; (row 2) MOSHE BRAKHA/ABC; LOCKWOOD/GLOBE PHOTOS; NICK BARATTA; CHRIS PIZZELLO/AP; (row 3) TAMMIE ARROYO/RETNA LTD.; CHRIS WEEKS/GETTY IMAGES; ALAIN ROLLAND/REFLEX NEWS; RICH SINGER/SILVER IMAGE; (row 4) DANNY TURNER; DAVID KEELER/ONLINE USA; RON DAVIS/SHOOTING STAR; LISA ROSE/JPI; (row 5) JIM SPELLMAN/WIREIMAGE; ALAIN ROLLAND/REFLEX NEWS; VIRGINIA SHERWOOD/ABC (soft cover only); NICK BARATTA/TEEN PEOPLE **TITLE PAGE** THOMAS E. FRANKLIN/BERGEN RECORD/CORBIS SABA **CONTENTS** (clockwise from right) SAM MIRCOVICH/GETTY IMAGES; BARON WOLMAN/RETNA LTD.; DOUG MILLS/AP

stories of the year

6-7 (from left) SPENCER PLATT/GETTY IMAGES; TOM HORAN/AP **8-9** (clockwise from top right) GULNARA SAMOILOVA/AP; SHANNON STAPLETON/REUTERS/GETTY IMAGES; JOSE JIMENEZ/GETTY IMAGES; STEVE HELBER/AP; SUZANNE PLUNKETT/AP; STEVE MCCURRY/MAGNUM PHOTOS **10-11** (clockwise from left) PATRICK ANDRADE/GAMMA; ED KEATING/NEW YORK TIMES; DAN CALLISTER/SPLASH; MATTHEW MCDERMOTT/CORBIS SYGMA **12-13** (clockwise from top right) BROOKS KRAFT/GAMMA; MIKE DE SISTI/AP; ELI REED/MAGNUM PHOTOS; PAUL FUSCO/MAGNUM PHOTOS; TIMOTHY FADEK/GAMMA; CAROL GUZY/WASHINGTON POST; TIMOTHY FADEK/GAMMA; MICHAEL SOFRONSKI/GAMMA **14-15** (clockwise from top right) WIN MCNAMEE/REUTERS/GETTY IMAGES; KENNETH LAMBERT/AP; STEVE MITCHELL/AP; JUSTICE DEPARTMENT/AP (2); ERIK FREELAND/SABA; ROBERT MECCA/AP; BRENNAN LINSLEY/AP **16-17** (clockwise from bottom left) BERLINER/BEI; RON SACHS/CORBIS SYGMA; KEVIN MAZUR/WIREIMAGE; KEVIN KANE/WIREIMAGE; NANCY KASZERMAN/ZUMA PRESS; KEVIN MAZUR/WIREIMAGE; TOM SPERDUTO/REUTERS/GETTY IMAGES; AP/CBS **18-19** (clockwise from top right) LARRY DOWNING/GETTY IMAGES; RICK WILKING/GETTY IMAGES; DOUG MILLS/AP; KEVIN LAMARQUE/REUTERS/GETTY IMAGES **20-21** (clockwise from top right) DAVID MCNEW/GETTY IMAGES; X17; LESLIE HASLER/AP; GARY HERSHORN/REUTERS/GETTY IMAGES; MICHAEL CAULFIELD/AP; SIPA PRESS; AXELLE/BAUER-GRIFFIN **22-23** (clockwise from top left) JAMES DEVANEY/BIG PICTURES USA; NICK UT/AP; JIM RUYMEN/REUTERS/GETTY IMAGES; NEWSMAKERS/GETTY IMAGES; JEAN CATUFFE/SIPA PRESS; KEVIN WINTER/IMAGE DIRECT; X17 **24-25** (from left) FRANK MICELOTTA/IMAGE DIRECT; LAWRENCE SCHWARTZWALD/SPLASH **26-27** (from left) STEPHEN J. BOITANO/AP; BART AHYOU/GETTY IMAGES **28-29** (from left) GLENN WEINER/IPOL; FAME PICTURES **30-31** (clockwise from top right) GAMMA; MISSISSIPPI SUN HERALD/AP; STEVE UECKERT/AP; ILKKA UIMONEN/GAMMA; JAMES THOMPSON **32-33** (from left) KATHY WILLENS/AP; DONALD MIRALLE/ALLSPORT; SYGMA

newsmakers

34-35 JEFF KATZ **36-37** (clockwise from top right) UK PRESS; FERRAN PAREDES/GETTY IMAGES; KENT GAVIN/WPA/AP; BIG PICTURES USA **38-39** (left) KEVIN

CREDITS PAGE: ERIC CHARBONNEAU/BEI

index

index